Kwasi Koranteng

The Cruel War

Illustrated by
Kevin Jones

Series editor: Rod Nesbitt

*For Leonard, Harriet, Sarah, Abenaa
and all my Liberian friends*

Heinemann International Education
a Division of Heinemann Publishers (Oxford) Ltd
Halley Court, Jordan Hill, Oxford OX2 8EJ

Heinemann Education Boleswa
PO Box 10103, Village Post Office, Gaborone, Botswana
Heinemann Educational Books (Nigeria) Ltd
PMB 5205, Ibadan

FLORENCE PRAGUE PARIS MADRID
ATHENS JOHANNESBURG MELBOURNE
SYDNEY AUCKLAND PORTSMOUTH (NH)
SINGAPORE TOKYO CHICAGO SAO PAULO

© Kwasi Koranteng 1993
First published by Heinemann International Education in 1993

British Library Cataloguing in Publication Data
A catalogue record for this book is available from the British Library

ISBN 0 435 89361 0

The right of Kwasi Koranteng to be identified as the author of this work has been asserted by him in accordance with the Copyright, Designs and Patents Act 1988.

Printed and bound in Great Britain
by Cox & Wyman Ltd, Reading, Berkshire

93 94 95 96 10 9 8 7 6 5 4 3 2 1

Chapter One

Maa had always been fat and full of energy. Now the civil war had reduced her to skin and bone. When she walked, it seemed she was carried along by the wind, not by her energy.

'Take it easy, Maa,' Paye comforted her. 'We won't die. I've been looking around for the past few nights. I'm going out again tonight.'

'How about your Louisa? Isn't she kind enough to bring us some food?'

'Maa, I don't think she has any food to spare, otherwise I'm sure she would bring us some. Have you forgotten she brought us kerosene?'

'Well.' Maa threw up her hands in despair and stood up. She walked to the backyard and sat under one of the shade trees. Soon, Paye heard her cracking palm kernels. That was what they were going to have for dinner.

At the beginning of the war, it had been easy to get *eddoe*, and *potanga*, a root similar to *eddoe*. Now they were difficult to come by as people had uprooted and eaten most of them.

A few weeks earlier, Maa had been forced to barter her sewing machine for a medium tin of 'gold dust', the new name for rice since the war had heated up. The seller insisted that she wanted property not money. The rice was finished and Paye and his people had to make do with palm kernel. Soon even that would be rationed.

There was no problem with water however. It was the rainy season, and every three days or so it rained. They could catch enough water from the roof to use. Besides, like many other Monrovians, they had dug a shallow well in the house. This also provided them with water.

Paye stood knocking at Paa's door. There was no answer. Paa was probably asleep, but he kept knocking. Paa might be sick, but it wasn't good for him to sleep all the time, Paye thought.

In spite of the war and the hunger it had brought, Paye still had firm muscles and looked very strong. He was about the height of his father, six feet tall. His mother was much shorter. At high school, everyone, including his teachers, called him 'Roman soldier' because of his muscular build and his smart walk. But he knew he was not cut out for the army. He preferred to use his energy for sports. He was a good footballer.

At the beginning of the war, many young Gio and Mano boys had taken up arms and joined the rebels. Paye refused to join them.

Paye had a handsome, friendly face, but he could be very rough, especially if someone tried to cheat him. He hated cheating. At school, he often went to the aid of the smaller boys when senior or bigger boys wanted to bully them.

'Come in,' a voice finally answered his knocks.

Paye walked in and sat by his father on the bed.

'How are you, Paa?'

'Not too bad, son, but I feel sick. I hope this hunger doesn't continue for long and that we'll get some food.'

'It won't, Paa. I'm sure I'll have something for us to eat soon.'

'How are you going to do that?'

'Never worry your head about that. There should be food soon.'

Paa sighed heavily.

'Look, Paa,' Paye went on, 'hunger is not the only cause of your sickness. I know you've been worrying over Dahn's death and the burnt road tanker. The harm has already been done. The sooner you get over it the better.'

'What you're saying is true, son,' his father replied, 'but it's very difficult to smile if, within a short time, you've lost your son and your only means of livelihood.'

'I understand that. We've all been worried, Paa. I think your sickness has affected Sonia too. If you get well she'll get well.'

'Hmm, thank you, son. You see, I've been thinking of the future too.'

'Paa, after the war I'm prepared to find work and help the family.'

'What happens to your university education?'

'That can wait for some time. First things first.'

'I love you for that, son,' Paa smiled, 'and I like your spirit.'

Paa felt much happier now. He knew his son would help as much as he could. The two of them talked for a while and then went out to sit by Maa in the backyard as she cracked the kernels. It was still safe enough in the yard.

It was curfew time. Paye's watch showed a little after midnight. He stepped out of his room and closed the door gently behind him.

He tiptoed to a corner of the dark sitting room. There he picked up a sack and a small axe. He already had half a candle and a box of matches in his pocket. He went out through the front door, again closing it gently behind him. Outside the main gate, he looked left and right and dashed along 19th Street. The street was dark and he tried to make as little noise as possible in his sneakers.

At the end of the street, he turned right and hurried on. Within a short time, he was far away from home. He went along a great many streets, avoiding the numerous roadblocks mounted by the rebels. Whenever necessary, he went over fences and through private compounds.

There was only a faint moon in the sky, and there were no electric lights. In the darkness that hung over the city, every Monrovian stayed behind locked doors. The power supply had been cut long ago. The sky was only lit up briefly whenever a rocket exploded or there was an exchange of gunfire between the army and the rebels.

Paye liked the darkness. He knew his way around without lights. He now vanished into an alleyway. He emerged halfway down another street. This street was littered with rotting human bodies. He slowed down and picked his way, careful not to step on any. They smelled horribly.

Paye walked close to the walls of the buildings, taking cover in their shadows. His empty stomach rumbled with hunger. Every now and then he took a quick look behind him. A few dogs lurked around, feasting on corpses. He shooed them away when they came too close. Vultures would have had a field day with the corpses, but vultures were a rare sight in the country now.

Soldiers and rebels could appear round any corner at any moment. They even hid in compounds and jumped out when people passed. He was lucky to have come so far, he thought.

As he looked left and right before crossing another street, a vehicle appeared not far away. Its guns spat bullets into the street corners. Paye dropped to the ground like a stone. He lay uncomfortably close to a rotting corpse.

The small pick-up passed by. Paye counted eight soldiers in the back, their sub-machine guns at the ready. A street fight erupted at the next corner. The pick-up had run into a rebel ambush. There was a fierce exchange of gunfire as the pick-up screeched to a halt.

The sub-machine guns cracked as they sprayed deadly bullets round. There were cries and moans as wounded men fell on the ground. Stray bullets smashed into walls and windows of nearby houses. A few whirled past Paye's ears. He felt a sharp pain on the temple. Warm blood oozed down his face. He wiped it and lay still again.

Then a grenade was tossed into the pick-up. The soldiers dived out and took cover. The pick-up exploded in a mass of flames and smoke. The flames lit up the surrounding area.

The fight continued for a few more minutes. When it stopped it had left almost all the soldiers dead and several rebels wounded.

A few minutes after the fighting had ceased, one of the bodies lying along the pavement suddenly came alive. It sprinted across the street. It was Paye. He was weak and hungry, but he managed a faint smile as he dashed into the safety of a deserted compound. He was panting like a dog. His sack, with the axe inside it, still hung over his shoulder.

For Paye, like many Monrovians, there was nothing strange in witnessing a street fight. Soldiers clashed with rebels on a daily basis. He had seen quite a few of them, especially during the past few nights when he had gone out hunting for food.

The place Paye now approached was the abandoned shop he had visited the previous night. Using the small axe, he broke in through the back door.

He lit the piece of candle he had brought along and inspected the shop. It had not yet been raided. A few tins of assorted foods still stood on the shelves. But he found no rice. He looked round again and saw a door. He quickly used his axe to smash the lock. It led into a small warehouse. The first thing he saw was a number of large sacks of rice lying on shelves. On other shelves were cartons of tinned foods.

Paye couldn't understand why there was so much to eat here while his family was starving to death. He used his axe again to open a tin of corned beef and scooped

The pick-up exploded in a mass of flames and smoke

the contents into his mouth. He washed it down with a bottle of soft drink.

He opened a sack of rice and divided it into two. He packed as many tinned foods and packets of sugar as he could carry on top of a half bag of rice and carried them away, taking his axe along. An hour later, he was back in the shop. This time he took the rest of the rice, more tins and a few batteries. He would need them for the radio and his torch.

Paye had been lucky. The Lebanese owner of the shop had fled with his family for Freetown in Sierra Leone. Before fleeing, however, he had removed the signboards. Otherwise soldiers or rebels would have noticed and raided the shop long ago.

◇

'Ha, Paye, you're back.' Maa sighed with relief in the dark sitting room. She was sitting in an armchair.

'You haven't been asleep, Maa?' asked Paye as he put the second lot of supplies down.

'I couldn't. I heard you come in and go out again and came to wait for you to return.' She lit a candle standing on the centre table. 'I've been praying for your safe return. What's that you've put on the floor?'

'Food, Maa.' Paye smiled and opened the sack for her to see. He removed his shirt and used it to wipe off the sweat on his body.

'God above be praised,' Maa said, crossing herself. 'You're wonderful,' she said happily.

'You haven't been to the kitchen?'

'No, why?'

'You'd have seen another sack of food there. Anyway, quickly boil some rice and wake up Paa and Sonia. They have something to eat now.' Paye carried the sack into the kitchen.

'We're lucky. We still have a little of the kerosene that Louisa brought,' Maa said as she hurried into the kitchen after Paye. She lit the kerosene stove and put some rice on to boil without washing it.

'I'm off to bed,' Paye said after he had drunk some water from the barrel and inspected the things he had looted from the shop.

'Why? Stay and eat before you sleep.'

'I've had something already. Make sure the others get some food.' Paye yawned as he walked out of the kitchen towards his bedroom. He had just done what a few daring young men did in Monrovia – ransacked a food shop in order to keep their families alive.

Paye was the second of his parents' children. He was twenty-five and he was studying computer engineering at the University of Liberia. The first child had been Dahn who had been killed earlier in the war. Sonia was the third and the last. Paye was the most intelligent and industrious among the children. Paa was counting on him to build a name for the family after he had finished university.

Unfortunately, the war had caught Paye in his second year at university, and the university, like all schools and colleges in Liberia, had been forced to close.

Paa had worked for many years as a transport officer with a shipping company in Monrovia. He had retired at an early age and used his retirement money to buy a road tanker on hire purchase. He carried petrol into the interior and brought food into the city in a hired truck. The food sold well and it had not taken him long to pay for the cost of the tanker.

It was out of his profits that he bought the house in which they lived. Their home was in a fine area where many businessmen and top public servants had houses.

Paa never brought his tanker to the house. He always left it in his elder brother's large compound in the northern area of Monrovia. Since the beginning of the war, Paa had not been able to move the truck. Then, early one morning, about two months after the war had started, his brother had braved the street fights to come to tell him the tanker was in flames. There had been a fight between soldiers and rebels, and a stray bullet had hit the fuel tank.

Paa had risked his life to go with his brother to see the tanker. When they got to his brother's compound, the tanker had already burned itself out. It had been a big blow to Paa. He had been a sick person ever since, and the death of his son made things even worse.

Chapter Two

'What's that?' Maa asked when Paye woke up late the next morning. He could hear gunfire and rocket explosions not very far away.

'I think the rebels are still trying to attack the Executive Mansion. Have Paa and Sonia eaten?'

'Twice already, since you went to sleep, and they've gone back to bed.'

'How are they?'

'Much better. But the kerosene is finished. Will you see Louisa and try to get us some more?'

'I don't know, Maa. What she brought was the only bit they could spare. Anyway don't worry.' He scratched his head and peeped out of a window. 'That wooden lottery booth is still standing. Good.'

'It's not ours,' Maa protested.

'Forget about that. This is wartime. If we don't take it, someone else will. Its owner may even be dead.'

Paye went outside. Soon he was straining every muscle to drag the heavy booth behind him into the backyard. He closed the gates and quickly cut it into pieces with an axe.

'Now you've a fine heap of firewood. Use it.'

'If it wasn't for you, I don't know what would happen to us,' Maa said as she made the fire in the yard. 'But I'm still not happy about that gunfire. They seem to be getting nearer to 19th Street. Can you feel how the ground is shaking?'

'We're safe here, Maa,' Paye assured her. 'I'm taking some rice to Louisa and her people. They may be starving by now.'

'By all means, but I hope you still don't have your eyes on that proud young woman,' Maa said.

'There you go again,' Paye grumbled.

'I know she gave you the kerosene, but I still see her as a proud, nagging woman. Besides her father is very mean. Since we came here he has always looked down on us, probably because we're not rich and don't have a car.'

'I don't think so, Maa. Maybe they're just reserved.'

'Don't forget they're Krahns and we're Manos. The war is now Krahns against Gios and Manos. We all know how people have betrayed others who do not belong to the same tribe. You must be careful with her. We have to think of our own survival. We're lucky they haven't betrayed us already.' Maa looked hard at her son.

'You've nothing to be afraid of,' Paye protested.

'Did you hurt yourself?' Maa asked, pointing to the fresh scratch on Paye's temple.

'I bumped into a wall in the darkness,' he lied. 'I'll be all right.'

'Well,' Maa shrugged, 'take the food to them. But I'm telling you that girl is not for you. My mother used to tell me that an orphan doesn't always look for the best things but just takes whatever will satisfy him.'

Paye ignored his mother. He filled a big polythene bag with a good quantity of rice and added four tins of sardines and a packet of sugar. He went to the front gate, looked around and ran over to one of the neighbouring houses. He knocked on the front door.

'Who's there?' a voice asked through a window.

'Me, Paye.'

'Aah, come in.' A young woman shot back the bolt, unlocked the door and opened it. She closed it quickly behind Paye.

Louisa was in the sitting room with her parents and three sisters.

Paye could see fear and misery in their faces. They had all lost weight. It was clear to Paye that in wartime it was not just hunger that made people thin. Fear and anxiety too made them thin.

'Here's some rice for you,' Paye said after greeting the family. 'We thought you might need it.' He handed the bag to Louisa.

The other girls crowded round Paye and Louisa and looked into the bag.

'Thank you,' they said in unison. They felt relieved to have Paye in their house.

'God bless you, young man,' Jim, Louisa's father, said. 'All the food we stocked up at the beginning of the war is finished.'

'How did you manage to get food at this time?' one of Louisa's sisters asked.

'Little sister, just eat it and forget where it comes from,' Paye answered, smiling at her.

'Paye, you don't seem to be much affected by the war,' Louisa said. 'You haven't lost much weight and you still look quite happy.' Louisa had grown very thin

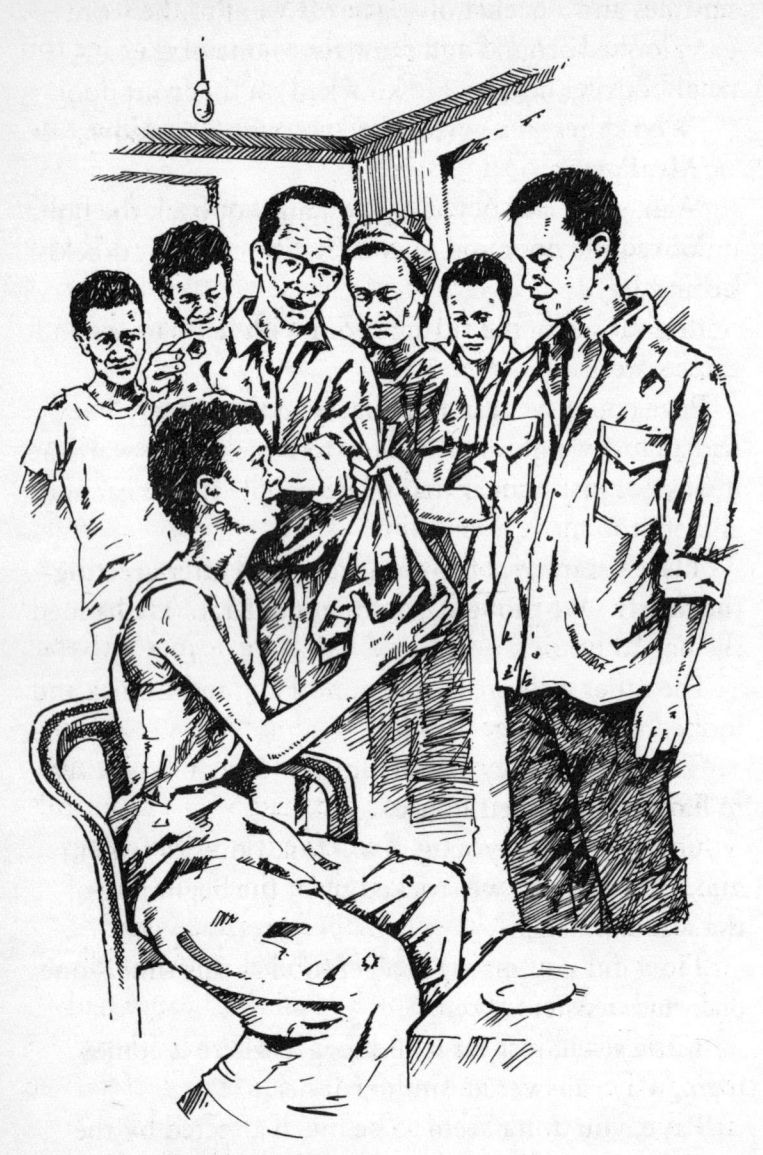

He handed the bag to Louisa

and she held her skirt in place with a safety pin.

'You're right. I don't allow the war to worry me too much,' Paye said.

'Why don't you come here more often and cheer us up?' another girl suggested.

'OK, girls, I'll come as often as possible to cheer —'

Suddenly there was a deafening explosion. As if at a command, everybody threw themselves to the floor and crouched behind the table and chairs with their hands clamped to their ears.

The explosion shook the house to its foundations and rattled the doors and windows. All the glass from the windows crashed to the floor.

Down on the floor behind the settee, Paye lay beside Louisa. Her large, brilliant eyes which had made Paye adore her so much had lost their sparkle. They now looked dull and worried and had gone deeper into their sockets. Paye knew she was afraid of the war.

For a moment he held her hand in his, patted it and smiled broadly at her. She only managed a weak smile.

Louisa, twenty-four years old, had been a beautiful young woman before the war. Five feet seven inches tall, she always stood very straight. She had a slim waistline, broad hips, well-shaped legs and large brilliant eyes in an oval face. Her black and abundant hair had been cut short. Much of all this beauty had now vanished because of the war and its hardships. Before the war she had worked as a private secretary in an oil company in Monrovia.

After some time, everybody stood up again. Louisa's sisters and her mother were weeping.

'Cheer up, everybody. Stop crying,' Paye laughed in spite of himself. 'Don't lose hope. We aren't going to die.'

Their faces brightened up a little.

'You know another reason we feel so bad, young man?' Louisa's father asked.

'Tell me, sir.'

'Did Louisa tell you that the rebels took our little car?'

'Yes, that was about two weeks ago.'

'That's correct. Yesterday they came for the Mercedes. It's one of my most treasured possessions. They broke open the garage door. At first I refused to give them the keys.'

'That could have been dangerous,' Paye remarked.

'Then they threatened us. I had no alternative but to give them the keys,' Jim ended sadly.

'It's a silly war really,' Paye said. 'We shouldn't have to suffer like this.'

'I hope your parents have recovered from the shock of your brother's death,' Doris said.

'That seems to have happened so long ago. I've cheered them up as much as I can.'

'I admire the courage you had to go and bury his body. You're a brave young man,' she added.

'I'm sorry we haven't been able to come and tell you how sorry we are,' said Jim. 'You know, because of the war on the streets, it's dangerous to step outside your front door even into your own compound. We'll come all the same.'

'Thank you, sir.'

'That's a really good boy,' Jim remarked when Paye had left.

'Yes, he is,' Doris added. How she wished she had a son like Paye. 'Girls, go and cook some of the rice for us.'

'I want to see what happened down the street,' Jim said and stood up.

'Take care, please,' his wife cautioned, 'and don't go into the street.'

◇

Paye and Louisa had become friends almost by accident. They had only been on greeting terms for a long time.

Then late one Saturday morning, Paye was coming from town when he saw a well-dressed family standing by their Mercedes-Benz car. From the way they were dressed, they were obviously going to a wedding. Their car had a flat tyre.

Jim did not want to make his suit dirty and crumpled and was looking for someone to change the tyre. Paye had promptly gone to their aid.

'Thank you, young man,' Jim said. 'Don't I know you from somewhere? Your face looks familiar.'

'Of course you know him, Dad,' Louisa said. 'He lives in our street.'

'Ah, yes,' Jim exclaimed. 'Well, thank you very much. We'll be seeing you then.'

And they had seen a lot of Paye since then.

Jim was a director of an aluminium company. Doris was a full-time housewife. The family was well off.

At first Jim had opposed the friendship between his eldest daughter and Paye, thinking that he came from a poor family. Doris had told him about how hardworking Paye's family was and the career he was pursuing. Jim had relaxed, even though he did not directly encourage the friendship. He wanted his daughter to marry early and he expected that sooner or later, the right man would come along.

As for Doris, once she saw that Paye was handsome and was going to be a computer engineer, he qualified to marry their daughter.

◇

In the safety of his father's compound, Paye peeped over the wall that faced the street. Part of the fourth house on his left across the street had been blown down and the roof had caved in. It appeared that the house had been abandoned before the blast. Lucky man, thought Paye. Perhaps he had taken the rebels' advice and left the city with his family before they arrived.

Paye could see a few heads peeping above the walls along the street. These days people dared not step out of their compounds. The only thing that drove them out was the search for food.

When he got back indoors, Maa was sitting in the room talking to Paa and Sonia, both of whom were better now. But Sonia had been terribly frightened by the explosion.

'You see what I told you, Paye?' Maa lamented. 'The fighting is right on our front doorstep.'

'It was a rocket which exploded,' Paye answered. 'It was meant for the Executive Mansion. Not for us. It has ruined the bank manager's house.'

'That means all the rockets and bullets fired at the Mansion can rain down on our heads,' Sonia moaned.

'No, little sister, this was just unlucky,' Paye said.

'I have a feeling we shall go through this war safely,' Paa said.

'That's right, Paa, we shall,' Paye agreed.

'God have mercy on us,' Sonia prayed.

'Louisa's people were grateful for the food,' Paye said, trying to divert attention from the war.

'That beautiful girl you've been dreaming of, you think she has eyes for you?' Maa mocked Paye.

'Aah, Maa, at least she likes my company.'

'Aaggh! She likes your company because you've carried rice to her and her people,' Maa sneered. 'After the war, she'll forget about you and go for a big man with a big car.'

'Maa, don't talk like that,' Paye said. 'They're nice people really. Ha! Why is your fire making so much smoke?' He looked into the backyard.

'That wood makes lots of smoke,' Maa said. 'It's probably the paint on it. I hope it doesn't attract the soldiers or rebels.'

'We can only risk it or starve to death,' Paye told her.

Paye had been thinking about the food he had collected. He searched Paa's old cupboard until he found a screwdriver, some nails, a hammer and a hinge. Inside his room, he climbed on top of his wardrobe and began to work on one of the ceiling boards.

'What are you doing?' Paa asked.

'Paa, you know that these people can burst in at any

time and carry away our precious stock of food.'

'So you're making an overhead store for it?'

'That's right,' Paye smiled at his father.

Some twenty minutes later, he had finished working on the ceiling board. The rectangular board now had a hinge on one end and could open upwards into the roof. There was hardly any sign that it had been turned into a secret door.

Paye went to the kitchen and poured some rice into a pan. He left that behind and carried the two bags of rice and other provisions into his room. He put them on the wardrobe. Soon, he had vanished into the ceiling. When he came out he was covered with dust and cobwebs.

'Maa, if any soldiers or rebels come here, tell them we've only a panful of rice left. Do you understand?' he said, dusting his clothes.

Maa nodded.

'Whenever you need anything, just tell me. I'll fetch it for you.'

'That's my boy,' Paa laughed lightly.

Paye was happy to see his father laugh. Paa had not laughed for a long time. Paa went to his room and came out holding a brown envelope. He gave it to Paye.

'That's the greater part of the money left in the house. It'll be safer up there.'

Paye vanished into the ceiling again. Paa heard two loud sneezes in the ceiling.

Chapter Three

'After seven months of brutal civil war in Liberia, six West African states have decided to send a peace-keeping force into that country. They will restore peace and order and supervise the return of the country to constitutional rule.'

'Hurray!' Paye shouted at the end of the radio announcement. Sonia, standing at the door, laughed in spite of her sickness. Paa too was overjoyed. He went to the back door.

'Maa, come and listen,' he shouted.

Maa rushed in.

'What is it?' she asked excitedly. 'Has the war ended?'

Paye told her about the announcement.

Maa danced for a minute as she always did when she was excited. But the joy that they all felt ended abruptly. There was a loud banging on the door.

'Everybody outside!' a hard voice shouted.

Several soldiers trooped into the compound. They wore olive green uniforms.

Paye turned off the radio which had been turned down low and pushed it into Paa's cupboard.

'Quick, get back to bed,' he whispered to Sonia.

Sonia went to her room and shut the door. Paye rushed into the compound with Maa and Paa. They knew that any delay would make the soldiers angry and they could start shooting.

The soldiers glared at them. Their leader was a short, stout man with a cruel face. They all held sub-machine guns. Their eyes looked as if they had smoked hashish.

'How many are there in the house?' the leader asked, pointing the muzzle of his gun at the front door.

'Four,' Paa answered. 'My daughter is sick in bed.'

'I said everybody out!' the leader yelled at Paa.

Paye ran inside. He came out carrying Sonia in his arms.

'Put her down.'

Paye obeyed. Sonia, still thin and sickly, pretended she could hardly stand. The soldiers did not have any sympathy for her.

'What are you cooking over there?' one of the soldiers asked, pointing at the smoke in the backyard.

'A little rice,' Maa said. 'Our last bit left.'

'That's all lies!' another soldier growled. 'It's always the last cup of rice. The war has made liars of you all.' He kicked the ground in anger.

'Come on, let's go and see,' the leader ordered.

Paa and Paye led the soldiers to the backyard and stood by the fire. One of the soldiers used the muzzle of his gun to lift the lid of the pan on the fire.

The leader nodded. 'You have food in the house, eh? We are under orders to collect all the food items in the area. Now take us inside and bring out whatever you have. Play any games with us and you'll suffer.'

They marched the family indoors. Two soldiers remained outside.

Inside, the soldiers searched the kitchen first and

then every room in the house. There was no food to be collected.

'My wife told you we're on our last cup of rice,' Paa told the soldiers.

'Yes, she did,' the leader said, smiling wickedly at Paa. 'In that case your son goes with us.'

'Spare him for me, please,' Paa pleaded, going down on his knees. 'The war has claimed one of my sons already. This is the only one left.' He knew that once they took Paye, he would be lucky to find Paye's body to bury. Maa joined him to plead with the soldiers.

'Well, what do you have for us?' the leader asked.

'Will you take some money?' Paa stood up.

'Make it quick!' one of the soldiers demanded angrily.

Paa hurried to his room and came back with fifty dollars. The leader snatched it and led his men away. 'We'll be back,' he said over his shoulder.

While his family went indoors, Paye went to peep over the wall that faced the street. What he saw made his heart miss a beat. 19th Street was bristling with soldiers in what seemed to be a big operation. Small groups of soldiers were moving from house to house, obviously searching for food. Some were carrying what looked like bags of rice and *gari* on their shoulders. Both ends of the road had been blocked by military trucks.

It was a quick operation. Within minutes, the soldiers had collected all the food they could gather from the houses on the street and climbed back into their trucks. They moved off at top speed.

If they came across any rebels on the way, there would be a brutal fight, Paye thought as he slipped back indoors. He did not tell the family what he had seen.

'What's all this nonsense?' Paa was saying, looking very miserable. Sonia was weeping.

'These men are using the war to commit all sorts of crimes,' Maa said. 'Paye, it's good you hid the rice in the ceiling. Stop crying, my dear.' She held Sonia in her arms.

'I've heard that they've been seizing people's food all over the place,' Paye said.

'Aaggh! It's a disgrace!' Maa exclaimed, shaking her head. She walked out to the backyard to see how the food was cooking.

'Paa, let's not get too worried about these things as long as we have food to live on,' Paye said, 'and Sonia, please stop crying. You're going to get better, don't worry.'

Paa nodded. 'Maybe we were foolish not to have escaped from Monrovia before the war got here.'

'Forget that, Paa. It's too late for us to blame ourselves. Nobody knew that the war would affect ordinary people this way,' Paye said.

Sonia went to her room. Paye brought the radio from the cupboard and turned it very low. He sat listening in with Paa for a long time.

By six o'clock that evening, Maa had finished preparing the family's second and final meal for that day. Since it was curfew time, they were now locked up in the house. Now at least they could afford two light meals a day. In the mornings they had rice porridge and sugar. In the evenings it was rice and sardines or some other tinned food.

To eat sardines at this time was a luxury indeed. Paye could scramble about like a monkey now, making frequent trips up to and down from the ceiling. Gradually they were beginning to regain their weight and energy.

After they had eaten, an unexpected visitor came in.

'Louisa!' Paye exclaimed in surprise. 'You didn't walk along the street all alone, did you?'

'I'm tired of being a prisoner in my own house,' she complained beside Paye on the old settee. 'How are all of you?'

'Still alive, thanks to Paye,' Paa answered.

'Did they come here?' Louisa asked Paye.

'They did. They were looking for food,' Paye said.

'Did they get anything?'

'Nothing,' Paye shook his head, 'so they wanted to take me along.'

'The crazy bunch!' Louisa fumed with anger. 'You did well to bring us rice and other things, but they took everything, even the rice we had just boiled to eat!'

'That means you've not eaten today?' Paa asked her.

Louisa shook her head. 'You've nothing to spare us?'

'I can get you a little rice later this evening,' Paye said.

'Thank you.'

Paye did not want to climb into the ceiling while Louisa was around.

'I'll tell you what, Louisa. What I brought you the other day was from a shop I raided. I made another trip

25

last night. I've cleared everything edible out of the shop now. I think there's only a few candles left.'

'Ha!' Louisa exclaimed. 'You mean you broke into a shop like the soldiers and rebels have been doing?' She was surprised as she gazed at Paye. 'That was where you got this scratch on your face, wasn't it?'

'Yes, it was made by a stray bullet.'

'So you told me a lie,' Maa accused Paye.

Paye laughed. 'I didn't want you to get frightened, Maa.'

'Weren't you afraid?' Louisa asked him.

'I don't know,' Paye shrugged, 'but I had to go, otherwise we would all starve to death. I'll bring you something soon.'

Louisa soon got up to leave.

'Sonia is sick,' Paye said when he got into the yard with Louisa. 'I think she has malaria. Can you get her some medicine?'

'I'll get you some medicine when you come.'

Outside the front gate, Paye looked left and then right, then he took hold of Louisa's hand and walked her to her compound.

'I'll be back.' He patted her on the shoulder and turned to go.

Louisa held him back. 'Paye, I'm afraid of the war.'

'I know. It shows in your eyes. Don't worry, I'm sure we'll live through it. The ECOMOG people are on their way here.'

'What's ECOMOG?'

'It's a West African peace-keeping force. It was announced on the radio.'

'We stopped listening to the radio long ago. There's no electricity and we've no batteries. Dad has a stand-by power generator, but there's no petrol. It's good news that peace-keepers are coming.' She smiled.

'I'll get you some batteries too. Go in and wait for me.' Paye watched as Louisa went in and locked the front door. He dashed over the street into his compound.

Through the window, Louisa watched him run off into the darkness. She really liked and admired him. He was strong and handsome and fearless. She wished she had a brother to comfort and protect the family.

Soon afterwards, Paye came back holding a pillow case filled with rice, a few tins of sardines and some dry cell batteries. He left with some chloroquine and vitamin tablets.

◇

It was later that evening. Maa was watching as Paye made Sonia swallow some of the medicine.

'It's thanks to that young woman,' Maa said, waiting to hear what Paye would say.

Paye did not say anything. He only turned and nodded at Maa with a smile.

'Don't deceive yourself, Paye. I know how young women behave today.'

'Maa, you watch. The war is bringing our two families closer together. Perhaps we'll marry one day.'

Maa sneered in disbelief. Paa went on listening to the radio. He made no comment.

Chapter Four

Paye was not used to staying indoors for days on end. He always had an excuse to go into the backyard as long as there were no soldiers or rebels on the street. Sometimes he fetched water from the shallow well and filled the barrel in the kitchen. If there was nothing to do, he just sat under a tree in the backyard.

Paye was loitering about the yard early one evening when he heard gunshots. The firing seemed to be coming from some distance away. He walked stealthily to the wall and peeped over it. There were soldiers on 19th Street again.

Two groups of soldiers were moving from house to house. One group advanced from his left and another from his right. They wore camouflage uniforms this time. Like the last time, they had blocked both ends of the street with their trucks. While the groups moved into different houses, single soldiers, posted all along the street, kept a lookout for rebels.

A cold sweat ran down Paye's back. The soldiers would certainly come to their house again. He stood there watching for some time. Then he dashed indoors and alerted his parents. Paa accompanied him back to the wall.

'What do you think they're doing, Paye?'
'Searching for food. The Executive Mansion must have run short of food again,' Paye replied. 'They seem

to be taking captives too, Paa, mostly young men like me. Look over there. There are four young men with their hands tied behind them. And look, that group on the other side has two.'

Paa made no answer. He pulled Paye back indoors.

'What is it?' Maa asked. She had been watching them through the window.

'Soldiers advancing down the street,' Paa said, trying not to frighten her or show her his own fear. 'Paye, the two houses next door are not occupied. Maybe we should move to one of them?'

'That'd be no help, Paa,' Paye said. 'They're combing every house on the street. They'd just find us there. Let's wait here for them.'

Sonia had heard the anxious conversation and the goings and comings. She came to join them. Maa told her what was happening.

'My God, what can we do?' Paa asked. His voice now showed all the anxiety and fear in him.

'We can only wait for them,' Paye repeated.

'If you join those unlucky boys there, nobody knows what will happen to you,' Paa said. Together with the others, he looked out of the sitting room window.

The soldiers had now entered Louisa's house. A few minutes later, Paa and the others saw her father talking to the soldiers on the street. They seemed to be questioning him hard and to be threatening him.

'Ha, Paa. Look, he's pointing,' Paye said, alarm sounding in his voice.

'Yes, you're right. He's pointing here. What can they be talking about?'

'I can't tell. Maybe about the food.'

Soon they heard the door of one of the neighbouring houses being smashed in.

'They'll soon be here,' Sonia said, breaking into fresh tears.

A few minutes later, soldiers walked into the compound.

'Everybody out here before I count to ten!' came a sharp order. 'One! Two!'

'Paye, what will we do?' Paa whispered nervously.

'Let's obey them.'

'Four!'

Paa shook his head. 'We'll go but not you. Climb up there,' he said, pointing to the ceiling. 'They'll kill you if —'

Paye stood there, unable to make his mind up.

'Seven!'

Paye watched as Paa pulled Maa and Sonia out with him.

'What are you people doing in there?' the leader asked as he glared at them with bloodshot eyes. He was the same person who had led a group of soldiers to the house the other time.

'Brother, we were getting our sick daughter out of bed,' Paa answered. 'You were here before. I remember your face.' Paa tried to pacify the soldiers.

'Yes, we were. You had food and you told us you had none,' the leader said sternly, ignoring Paa's smile.

'I didn't tell lies, brother,' Paa tried to explain. 'There was nothing but rice on the fire.'

'Still telling lies, huh? You didn't have food, yet your

son carried food to the people in that house.' The leader cocked his thumb towards the street.

'Where is that young man?' another soldier snarled.

'He's not in the house,' Paa replied.

'Sure?'

'Sure, brother. He left the house in the morning without telling us. I think he's gone to look for something to eat.'

Maa thought they were lucky this time as there was nothing cooking in the backyard. Neither was there a single grain of rice in the kitchen. They had eaten early today. But that was not to be.

'Stop the lies, man!' the leader snapped. 'You have food in this house!'

Paa held his hands palms upward to show there was nothing.

'You're Manos, aren't you?' the leader asked Paa angrily.

'Yes, but we're brothers, aren't we?' Paa had begun to sweat heavily. He did not like this talk about ethnic groups.

One of the soldiers shook his head. 'If we're your brothers, you should share your food with us,' he accused Paa.

'If we had food, we would share with you,' Maa pleaded. 'You can come to the kitchen and see. There's nothing.'

'Shut up, woman!' the soldier screamed at Maa. 'I was talking to your husband.'

'We're telling you the truth, brothers,' Paa said in pleading tones.

The leader levelled his gun at Paa. 'You people are still making fools of us and for that —' He didn't finish what he was saying.

Two shots rang out in quick succession.

'A-a-a-h.' A long scream died in Paa's throat as he held his chest and slumped to the ground.

Two more shots rang out.

'Aah! Paye-e-e!' Maa yelled as she crashed on top of Paa.

A single shot followed. Sonia sank to the ground without a sound as blood spouted from her throat. Blood from the three formed little pools on the ground.

Then the soldiers stormed into the house. First the kitchen, then the store, then they went into Paa's room. There was no food to be found.

In their anger, they broke wardrobes and boxes. They looted whatever money and valuables they could find. They smashed the television set and pushed the refrigerator over.

'That boy's lucky we didn't get him,' one of them said.

'Never mind. We'll get him another time,' the leader replied.

Still angry, they stormed out of the house mouthing curses and insults and leaving behind death and destruction. Outside the front door, one of them savagely kicked Paa's lifeless foot out of the way.

Up in the ceiling above his room, Paye was sweating. He had heard the shots and the cries of Maa and Paa as the bullets ripped into them.

A long scream died in Paa's throat as he slumped to the ground

'Oh no... no... no,' he moaned, slapping his head as he lay on the beams. Have they been wounded or killed? he wondered.

He did not hear any cries from his sister. Perhaps they had spared her, he thought. He started to descend, meaning to attack the soldiers. Then he stopped himself. It would be sheer madness to attack armed and bloodthirsty soldiers.

Then he heard the soldiers as they stormed into the house and smashed up things. He even heard them swearing and cursing in his room as they overturned his bed and sent it crashing to the floor. If they looked up at the ceiling and got suspicious, he was finished, he thought.

The sweat that poured down Paye's body was not caused by the heat trapped inside the ceiling. It was caused by fear and anxiety, and by hatred. He kept listening. He heard retreating boots and more curses and insults. Then all was quiet.

Paye waited until he was sure that the soldiers had left. Then he opened the trapdoor and climbed slowly down on to the wardrobe.

What he saw in the yard made him stagger against the front door. But he steadied himself. His family had been reduced to lifeless bodies. Maa half-lay on Paa, as if to protect him. All three had looks of agony on their faces. Their blood was still oozing on to the ground.

'So this is what they did to you, Paa?' he spoke sadly to the corpse. Tears bathed his face as he bent over the bodies and sobbed out loud.

After some time he very gently picked up the bodies

and laid them at the back of the house. Then he went indoors and wept again. He did not know how long he wept.

'Paye! What's happening?' the girl's voice sounded genuinely disturbed.

Paye raised his head. Through hazy eyes he saw Louisa standing above him.

'We heard gunshots. What happened? And why is there blood on the ground outside?' Louisa asked again.

'They're all dead, shot by soldiers,' Paye moaned, pointing at the backyard. He stood up slowly.

'You mean killed?' Louisa asked in a horrified voice. She began to weep.

'Come and see.' Paye pulled her violently to the backyard. 'Here they are,' he said bitterly, 'the victims of your father's betrayal.'

Louisa felt dizzy. Her body went limp and she began to sink to the ground.

Paye got hold of her and carried her limp body inside. He put her on the sitting room floor and fetched a rag and a bowl of water. He began to wipe her face. She was soon conscious again.

Louisa sat up weakly. She was very pale.

'What will we do now?' she asked, looking into his face.

'Nothing,' he said, 'except bury them and keep on living.' He felt confused. He was sad and angry but also sympathetic towards Louisa at the same time.

It was now quite dark. Paye went into Maa's room and brought out three pieces of cloth. From the storeroom he got a shovel and a pick-axe. He walked to the backyard. Louisa followed him and offered to help wrap up the bodies.

'No, please,' he said, glaring at her with red eyes. 'Go home. I can bury them alone. Your people might be looking for you!'

'Why are you angry with me?'

Paye did not answer her. He took the pick-axe and measured the ground. Louisa took the shovel. She was determined to help.

Luckily the ground was not very hard. It had rained a few days earlier. As Paye dug, Louisa shovelled out the soil. It was risky even to dig a grave to bury a dead relative in a compound. If soldiers or rebels appeared, they would be in trouble for breaking the curfew. Paye dug as hard as he could.

In an hour they had prepared three shallow graves. Paye put the bodies in the graves and said a short prayer. His tears mingled with the earth as he covered up the bodies.

'Thank you. Good night,' he told Louisa curtly as he gathered the tools and walked indoors.

It was most strange that he should behave like this and did not bother to walk her home. Louisa couldn't quite remember the last thing Paye had said before she had fainted. But definitely there was something wrong. What was it? She thought as hard as she could as she walked towards her house.

Chapter Five

'Louisa, where have you been all this time?' Jim questioned his daughter angrily when she got back. 'You know it's dangerous to leave the house.'

Louisa did not answer immediately. Jim noticed that her eyes were red with crying and she looked very pale.

'What's happened?' he asked her more gently.

'Those gunshots we heard, they've killed Paye's family.'

'Oh no!' her parents exclaimed simultaneously. 'You mean they've killed all of them?' Doris asked.

'Yes, all except Paye.'

'Why did they kill them?' Jim asked, puzzled.

Louisa shrugged. 'I don't know. I didn't ask him and he didn't tell me.'

'These soldiers and rebels! This war!' Jim exclaimed, stamping his feet angrily on the floor.

'We … we've buried the bodies – his father, mother and sister Sonia.' Louisa burst into fresh tears. Her sisters joined her.

'You mean it?' Jim asked, still not sure about what she had told them.

'Yes.'

'Where?'

'In their compound.'

'Oh, that poor boy,' Doris said as tears ran down her cheeks.

'I wish I could go and console him,' Jim said.

'Not tonight, please, it's too dangerous,' Doris warned. 'Not with those mad soldiers and rebels on the streets.'

'I'll go tomorrow then. Stop crying now, girls.'

◇

The rain which fell that night calmed people's nerves. It allowed them to sleep a little better, in spite of the war. But not Paye. He was deeply troubled. Throughout the night he paced up and down the house. He wrung his hands in misery and talked to himself, as if he was out of his mind. It was a night of great mental agony.

By the morning, he had decided what to do. He could no longer stay in this house. He could not bury his family in the compound and then draw water in the same compound to drink.

In any case there was no safety here. The soldiers could burst in again at any moment and finish him off. That would mean the end of his family.

And there was nobody to talk to. The immediate neighbours had left Monrovia several months previously. The only neighbours he could talk to had turned traitors. If he stayed here, he would go mad with loneliness and sadness.

◇

'Dad, where are you going to?' Louisa asked her father the following morning. She knew where he was going, and she had been watching him put on his shirt and buckle his sandals.

'To see the young man.'

'I'm going with you.'

'You stay here,' Jim said in an unfriendly tone. 'Let me go and see him first.'

'I'm going with you,' Louisa insisted.

'Well, if you are not afraid.'

They walked quickly across the street towards Paye's compound. The front door had been locked. The back door too. But when Louisa reached up above the door and felt along the door frame, she felt the key. She turned the key and they went in.

'Paye!' she called out in the sitting room. Only the empty house echoed her voice faintly.

'Where are you?' Louisa's voice sounded more anxious than before.

The house echoed her voice again. The walls and broken furniture seemed to stare back at them.

'I don't like the look of this place,' Jim said. 'This broken furniture, who did it all?'

'I'm sure it was the soldiers.'

'Paye!' Jim called out.

'I don't think he's in the house. Let's go,' he said after they had shouted his name a few more times.

'Let's look a bit more, Dad.' The bedrooms had all been locked, but Louisa searched the kitchen, the storeroom, the toilet and the bathroom.

When Louisa had finished searching the house, they went to look around the compound. It was all in vain.

'These are the graves,' she told her father.

'It's terrible,' he remarked, 'that the war should destroy such innocent lives. We must go. I trust wherever Paye is, he is safe and can take care of himself.' He held his daughter's hand as they went out of the compound.

Louisa was sad and quiet throughout the day. She would not even eat her ration of the boiled rice.

◇

'Halt!' the rebel ordered the man who limped past the roadblock on a crutch.

The lame man stopped and leaned on his crutch. He stared at the rebels. There were about ten of them at the roadblock. Their eyes were blood-red and they all held sub-machine guns. Some of them looked very young, as young as eleven or twelve. But they did not look any kinder or friendlier than the older ones.

'Where are you going?' one of them asked the lame man, pointing the gun at him.

'To the nearest clinic or hospital,' the lame man answered in a sickly voice.

'What for?'

'To seek shelter and medicine. They blasted the roof off my house and injured me.'

'Where do you live?'

The man told them.

The rebels stared at him. His left leg was bent back almost double and looked swollen. It had been tied with a dirty rag. The man's shirt was faded and crumpled and his hair was very untidy. Sweat was pouring down his body. He looked pale and hungry.

He also looked really sick from the wound on his leg. His face showed that he was in enormous pain.

One of the rebels looked at the lame leg.

'Remove the rag!' he ordered in a cold voice.

The lame man bent down and tried to remove the rag. He winced with pain. 'It's stuck in the wound.'

'Remove it!' came the order again.

The man tried again and gave up. He could not bear the pain.

'He looks like a soldier in disguise,' another rebel said. 'You remember the case of the lame man who was allowed through the roadblock on Broad Street? He turned round only to throw a grenade at our men. Be careful with this man.'

'Ahaa!' another rebel exclaimed, 'what's this under your arm?'

'Just a little rice,' the man said, showing them the food he carried.

A rebel frisked him quickly. He found nothing.

'You're a Krahn man, aren't you?' he asked.

'No, brother,' the lame man answered, 'a Mano like you.'

In quick succession one of the rebels rattled out three questions in Mano. The lame man answered back quickly in the same language.

'OK, move on.' The rebels turned their attention to a group of people approaching the roadblock.

As the man limped along, he saw other people walking or limping towards a clinic. Others were being carried in wheelbarrows. Still others were being carried on someone's back. These were the people who had been wounded in the recent fighting. The open wounds that some had were too ugly to look at. There was suffering on every face. Too many innocent people had suffered in this war, the lame man thought.

Some of the houses in the street had had their roofs blown off. The mortar shells and rockets had caused a lot of damage. Bullet marks could be seen on the walls of the buildings. Doors had been smashed and glass windows shattered. The streets were littered with burnt-out vehicles. Corpses lay in the streets rotting. How they smelled!

The lame man limped along on his crutch, looking pale and sickly and hungry. Every hundred yards or so he stopped and rested a little.

Once inside the compound of the Lutheran church, Paye threw down his makeshift crutch. He sat under a tree to recover his breath and to straighten and massage his left leg.

He was tired from the long walk in the hot sun. Using the crutch had made his progress slow and difficult. His left armpit itched. The skin was raw with the rubbing of the crutch.

There were many people inside the huge compound. In addition to the magnificent church, there was a big two-storey school and other buildings.

Some of the people were cooking in the compound. Others slept under trees and on the verandas of the church and school block. There was a huge pile of chairs, benches and tables outside.

Having rested, Paye walked to a group of young men talking under a tree.

'Brothers, where are the Red Cross people?' he asked them.

'There's no Red Cross here,' one of them answered.

'I heard there were Red Cross workers to give food and medicine to the refugees who came here.'

'That's not true,' another man said. 'We have to take care of ourselves.'

'Oh well,' Paye shrugged, looking around. 'Are you safe here?'

'So far. This is supposed to be a holy place,' a short man answered. 'We're sure the fighters will respect the church. I don't think they'll come and make trouble.'

'OK, thank you.' Paye strolled into the church. People had spread out mats and cloths and were sleeping. Some just sat idly talking or sewing, while a few prayed at the altar.

Paye now understood why the benches and other furniture had been stacked outside. The church was now one big dormitory for war refugees.

He walked to the school block. The picture there was the same.

There were children, young and old women, women with babies, and pregnant women too. There were a few men, both young and old. They formed quite a crowd. They all hoped that they would be safe here and that the war would end soon.

Paye now felt very thirsty. He begged a cup of water from a nursing mother. Then he went back to the church. Suddenly he felt very tired. He stretched out on the floor, using his small bag of rice as a pillow. As soon as his head touched it, he sank into a deep sleep.

Chapter Six

It was ten days since Paye had vanished from the neighbourhood. Louisa had never been herself since the war began. But with the disappearance of Paye, life had become worse for her.

She was always sad and gloomy now and kept mostly to herself. She no longer bothered to join in the conversations of her sisters and parents. Her father had somehow managed to bargain for a small bag of rice and the food ration was a little bigger now.

Louisa ate only half her ration. Her appetite had gone with Paye. She sat staring straight in front of her, as if there was a nagging thought on her mind.

She had noticed that her father had been restless for some time now, though he did not want to show it. Was it fear and anxiety? Was it a feeling of guilt? she wondered. She had been trying, without success, to remember what Paye had told her the day his family was shot. 'Your father, your father, your father…' Those were the only words she could recollect and they kept echoing in her head. What about her father?

Paye was not around to make them laugh any more. He was nowhere to be found. Two or three times every day, she sneaked out to see if he was back. Every day she found the house empty.

On the morning of the tenth day, she sneaked out as usual. She walked quickly down 19th Street, making enquiries as she went along.

At last she came to her friend Sarah's house.

'Sarah, how's the war treating you?' she asked.

'Badly, Louisa,' she answered. 'Look how thin I've become. What are you doing so far from home? Looking for something to eat?'

'No, I'm looking for Paye. Have you seen him?'

'Ye-es, I have.' Sarah nodded slowly. 'But it was a few days back. He had been hit in the leg with a bullet or something.'

'Oh no, not Paye,' Louisa said, giving a gasp.

'He was limping on a crutch.'

'Limping? But he was not hurt when the soldiers attacked his house.'

'Aah! Tell me what happened.'

Louisa told her friend the bad news. 'But he wasn't hurt,' she added. 'You're sure you saw him?'

'Yes, with my own eyes, on this very street.' She pointed.

'Did you talk to him?' Louisa asked in a worried voice.

'I did, but he didn't answer me, strangely enough.'

'Thank you, Sarah.' Louisa turned back to the street.

'Aren't you going home?' Sarah asked.

'No, I've got to look for him,' Louisa answered over her shoulder.

'It's dangerous for a woman to walk around alone. Go back home!' Sarah cried after her.

She looked at her friend running down the road, and shook her head. Louisa would be lucky to survive the day. The war had made her sick in the head, Sarah thought, as she closed the door.

◇

It was a few minutes to six that same evening. And it was almost curfew time. Everybody was supposed to be off the streets. After six only armed soldiers and rebels roamed the streets.

Jim had been worried the whole day. His eldest daughter was nowhere to be found. He had been bold enough to ask at every house on the street. At two places he had been told Louisa had come to ask about Paye.

'I don't know what's wrong with your daughter,' he fumed at Doris.

'Jim dear, don't you be getting angry with me,' Doris said. 'I haven't spoken with her and she hasn't told me anything. You know how quiet she has become.' She was as much disturbed about Louisa as her husband.

'What madness has got into her?' Jim asked himself.

'Louisa will come back,' Doris comforted herself. 'She'll come back.'

'But it's curfew time and that's what worries me all the more. If she's not dead by now, coming home is going to be a real problem. Being a woman, they can kill her, they can —' The rest of the sentence died in his throat.

'Don't talk of death,' his wife protested.

'This girl will be the death of me!' Jim stamped his foot on the carpet. 'That young man must have cast a spell over her.'

'Haa!' Doris exclaimed with surprise.

'Otherwise how can you explain her behaviour?' Jim went on.

He went to the street again to look up and down. There was not a single person in sight.

◇

Louisa was among a large crowd heading for the nearby Catholic hospital. A group of rebels were checking identity cards before allowing people to go through a roadblock.

It was a few minutes to six. Louisa was terribly tired and her body was coated with dust. It had been a long, tiring search. She had learnt that people took refuge in hospitals and churches where they thought they would be safe. She had asked at as many churches and clinics as she could. She had come across a few Payes but never the one she was seeking.

Louisa looked at the long queue in front of her. The sky had begun to darken. After six o'clock, the rebels checking identity cards might not allow them to pass. Then the crowd would be locked between two roadblocks. Nobody knew what might happen before six o'clock the following morning. Louisa stepped out of the queue and moved forward.

'Get back!' a bearded rebel barked at her.

She walked on.

'Back, I told you!' the rebel ordered as he took a step forward and levelled his rifle.

All eyes were now on Louisa. She went forward and pushed her way past the rebels checking the ID cards.

The bearded rebel blocked her way.

'Who are you?' he asked threateningly.

'Louisa.'

'You think we're just playing games, checking ID cards here?'

'I'm looking for my brother,' she said, not answering the question. 'I don't have an ID card.'

'Then go back!'

'Sorry, sir, but I have to find him,' she burst out, shaking her head.

'Look, woman, this is wartime,' the rebel said, glaring dangerously at her, 'and you'd be safer if you were polite to anyone with a gun, you under —'

'I don't care about your war,' she cut in angrily. 'All I want is my brother and I'm going to look for him!'

The rebel cocked his gun.

'For the last time get back!'

The crowd watched fearfully. They knew it was the end for the young woman.

'I'm not going back!' Louisa screamed at him. 'We're fed up with this war. When will we have peace? When is this killing going to stop?'

With that she stepped around the rebel and walked quickly away, daring them to shoot her.

Four rebels stood with their guns at the ready. It was easy for them to shoot. But somehow, their fingers felt too stiff to press the trigger.

'The girl's mad,' the bearded rebel said, tapping a finger on the side of his head.

'No, she's not mad,' another rebel said calmly. 'Perhaps it's we who are mad. Come on, remove the roadblock and let the people pass.'

The roadblock was pushed aside. The crowd rushed

past, happy that Louisa had made the crossing easy for them. Many among them had lost their ID cards.

A little after six o'clock, Louisa wearily entered the compound of the Catholic hospital.

'Sister, is this your first time here?' a woman asked.

'Yes.'

'Come with me.' She took Louisa's hand and led her along. 'You look hungry, I've got some food.'

Louisa accompanied the woman to one of the hospital wards. It was crowded with people. Three children ran to embrace the woman.

'My children,' the woman told Louisa. 'Their father was shot by rebels right in front of our house.'

'Sorry, my sister,' Louisa comforted her.

'Please sit here.'

The woman arranged two small boxes and a few cooking pans in a corner. That was all the property she and her children had left. Tired, Louisa gladly sat on one of the boxes and drank the water the woman offered.

'There's some rice porridge here.' The woman spooned some into a pan for Louisa. 'I'm afraid it's cold and there's no sugar.'

Louisa grabbed the pan and tilted it to her lips. It was empty by the time she put it down.

'Thank you, sister,' she said.

'So your brother is missing?' the woman asked her as she seated herself beside Louisa on the other box.

'Yes, it's been ten days now.'

The woman looked hard into Louisa's eyes. She could read worry and anxiety there.

'It's going to be difficult to find him,' she said sympathetically. 'Better stop searching and go home.'

'I have to look for him,' Louisa said in a determined voice.

'Well, I admire the great courage you showed at the roadblock. Perhaps that courage and determination will help you to find him.'

Louisa nodded in agreement. 'I'm really angry with this war,' she said.

As they talked, Louisa's eyes roamed the ward. It was crowded with the sick and wounded as well as those just trying to escape the war. All the beds were occupied. In between the beds, people had spread mats and pieces of cloth.

'Sister, the earlier I begin to search, the better,' she told the kindly woman. 'I'll be back. Thank you very much.'

She began in the wards. A few people had lit candles. She searched patiently, from bed to mat, ward to ward, from veranda to veranda, peeping into faces and asking questions as she went along.

By midnight, Louisa had still not found Paye. She was afraid that Paye was not there. She went back to the woman who had given her food and stretched out beside her in the corner.

When the woman woke up the next morning, Louisa was nowhere to be found.

Chapter Seven

'Don't you think we should find a way of protecting ourselves here?' Paye asked his new friend. The two of them sat on the veranda of the church scraping and eating a coating of hard rice at the bottom of the pan.

'What kind of protection are you thinking of?' his friend asked.

'We could use the benches and tables to barricade the doors at night.'

'You think that would work against bullets and mortar shells?' his friend wondered.

Paye shrugged and forgot about the matter. There were always lots of people to talk to. For Paye, talking to people meant sharing his burden with them and that gave him some relief. Many of the people had lost their families just like him. Paye began to feel more relaxed.

The distance from home also made the death of his family a bit less painful. Once in a while he still shed tears.

Later that afternoon, he was washing his hands when he heard his name echoing inside the church. He rushed in. There, standing in the middle of the church calling out his name, was Louisa.

He stopped and stared in surprise. Then he walked slowly towards her.

'Louisa!' He held out his hands. When she saw him she began to cry with relief. Then she started to shiver and she collapsed with hunger and exhaustion. He carried her out to the veranda and brought some water.

'Aren't you happy to see me?' she asked after regaining her strength.

'I ... I am,' he answered slowly.

'No, you're not.'

'I am, Louisa. It's only that I'm surprised. Have all your family been killed too?'

'No,' she shook her head, 'they're alive.'

'Then what brings you here?'

'You.'

He stared at her. 'Me?'

'Yes.'

'You must be crazy, Louisa, to take such a risk.'

'I had to. Something drove me to look for you.'

Paye was puzzled. Then he remembered Louisa must be hungry. He asked his friend to put a little rice on the fire.

'How did you know I was here?' he asked her.

'I've been searching since yesterday morning.' She told him about her experiences.

'That was very brave,' Paye remarked, 'but it was foolish bravery. It could have brought another death on my hands.'

'Paye, aren't you just happy to see me now?' she asked him again.

The question cut deep into Paye.

'Yes, yes I am, Louisa.' This time there was no hesitation in his voice.

After Louisa had eaten, Paye got her a bucket of water for her to wash herself. Then they went to the veranda and sat close together talking. She talked about the war and her father's anxiety for the family. She talked about the worries that had driven her to look for him. They talked until it began to get dark.

Louisa was tired, but the sight of Paye made her excited and drove the sleep from her eyes. They conversed deep into the night.

When at last they went to sleep, the cool parts of the church were all occupied. They had to go behind the altar, where the air was rather stuffy, to find a place.

They had no mats or cloths. They just stretched out on the floor. Both of them fell into a deep satisfying sleep.

That night, the soldiers came, like midnight hunters.

◇

It had been a quiet night, quiet because there was no fighting nearby, although there was the usual firing of guns and mortars in the distance.

Inside the church, a hungry baby woke up and felt for its mother's breast. The young mother thrust the nipple into the hungry baby's mouth. The baby sucked, but there was no milk. The breast had gone dry.

Some refugees were snoring. Children tossed about in their sleep. A few people were having nightmares. The hungry baby howled for its mother's milk.

'Keep that child quiet,' an old lady said sleepily nearby. The young mother put the other nipple into the baby's mouth. The baby lay quietly. What was that humming noise? the mother wondered as she blinked fully awake.

The noise came nearer and nearer, then right into the compound of the church. She gathered up her cloth around her and sat up, still suckling the baby. There were trucks in the yard. Their headlamps had lighted up the whole place. Some of the refugees had begun to stir awake.

The woman stood up and picked her way to the door. There must have been a dozen army trucks and jeeps. They beamed their headlights on the church and the school block. Soldiers were jumping down from the trucks and taking up positions in the yard.

The woman dashed along the veranda towards the back of the church, clutching her baby to her chest. A single shot rang out, tearing through mother and baby.

'A-a-i-i!' the woman screamed as she fell to the ground with her baby.

Inside the church, people had been shocked out of their sleep. Confusion and fear were clearly written on their faces as the armed soldiers entered the building and turned their flashlights on the refugees.

People looked left and right for a way to escape. There was none. Some of the windows had been shut. The open ones and all the doors had been blocked by soldiers holding guns and wearing masks.

Then an order rang out.

'Fire!'

Bullets tore into bodies. The dead and wounded fell heavily to the floor. There were so many that some fell on others. Many collapsed from sheer terror.

'Have mercy! Spare our lives!' hundreds of voices cried out to the soldiers. Mothers clung desperately to their babies. Children shrieked in fear. Young men and women tried to find a way out. Old men and women moaned, not knowing what to do. But there was no mercy from the guns.

Blood splattered on the floor and walls. People slipped and fell, tripping others in the process. Mothers fell, still holding their babies. Pregnant women, with bullets in chest and stomach, tumbled to the floor. The bullets did not spare men, women or children that night.

Behind the soldiers' masks, eyes gleamed with satisfaction as the bullets hit their mark. And behind the masks there was no pity. Only the desire to finish the night's assignment as quickly as possible. It was a dark assignment indeed, one they would not talk about afterwards.

'Fire! Fire!' the order came repeatedly. 'Kill! Kill them all!' The powerful voice of the commander barked out the order.

A few men and women tried to force their way out through the windows. They only got halfway. The soldiers in the yard cut them down, leaving their bodies dangling from the broken glass.

In the school building, a similar massacre was taking place. People tried to jump from upstairs windows to safety. Shot in mid-air, they were dead before they hit the ground.

Paye was in a deep sleep when the noise of gunshots and piercing cries hit his ears. What was all this? He knew the answer the moment he opened his eyes. The church was under attack. His first reaction was to reach

The bullets did not spare men, women or children that night

out for Louisa. There was no time even for that. Someone stepped on his stomach. Another fell on him. He did not have a chance to push off the dead body. More people tumbled on top of him.

'Save me, Paye!' That was all he heard from Louisa as a dead body crashed down on her.

The bodies kept piling on top of them. In a short time they were trapped under a mass of dead and struggling bodies.

Then the firing stopped, but only for a moment.

'The wounded and the moving, get them all!' came the sharp order.

There was another storm of bullets as the soldiers now aimed at people moving or groaning on the floor.

When the firing stopped, there was not a single refugee moaning or moving inside the church. By then the operation inside the school building had also ended. The soldiers scrambled into their trucks and moved off at top speed. The church compound was plunged back into darkness and silence.

Under the mass of bodies, Paye was still alive. But he was suffocating. How could he free himself from this mountain of bodies? The weight was too great. All the time, blood was pouring over his face and body.

He was lying on his back. It was difficult to push upwards, just using his arms and knees. Gradually he managed to turn around. With his elbows on the floor, he pushed as hard as he could. With a coating of blood on them the bodies began to slip off.

He heaved again. More bodies fell off. He was free. He gasped for breath. There was no time to waste. He began pulling at bodies where he knew Louisa lay.

'Louisa, Louisa,' he called. There was no answer. He redoubled his efforts. He pulled off more bodies.

Someone groaned weakly on the floor. He took hold of Louisa's waist and pulled. Soon she too was free. As he carried her to the veranda, he heard a woman moaning.

Paye put Louisa down on the veranda and went back. He removed more dead bodies. Five minutes later, he had saved a pregnant woman.

Back on the veranda, he got a little water and washed the blood off his body. He couldn't do anything about the blood stains on his clothes.

Early in the morning, soon after the curfew ended, the three of them set out from the church compound. They were probably the only survivors of the massacre. They parted company with the pregnant woman at the first road junction.

'Where are you coming from with all this blood on you?' a rebel asked them at a roadblock.

'The church over there,' Paye said. 'Soldiers came in the night. They tried to kill all the refugees. Go and see the bodies piled up there for yourself.'

'You two are lucky then,' the rebel said and waved them through.

'What a pity a place of worship should be turned into a slaughter house,' Louisa said as they went along.

'We were saved only because we were at the back of the altar. Do you realise that?' Paye asked her.

She nodded.

By noon they were safely back home.

Chapter Eight

'Look! They're back,' Jim exclaimed through the window when Paye and Louisa entered the compound. He opened the front door for them.

'Were you two in a pool of blood or something?' Jim sounded very angry as he spoke. He looked tired and worn out, as if he had not slept for weeks. He stared at the pair who stood just inside the doorway.

'We've just come from the Lutheran church,' Paye said. 'There was a terrible massacre there last night.'

'And you returned from the dead?' Jim asked in his fury. He had been certain his daughter was dead.

Doris and the girls had crowded around them and were looking at them as if they were ghosts.

Paye told them briefly what happened. They were all horrified.

'Well, at least they are back,' Doris said gratefully, trying to calm her husband's anger.

'Sir, have the soldiers been here in the past few days?' Paye asked Jim.

'Only once since you vanished,' Jim growled.

'Thanks. I think I'd better get back to the house,' Paye said. He turned to Louisa. 'Maybe I'll see you later.'

'Doris, please take this runaway girl to the boy's quarters and give her a bath before she comes in here,' Jim told his wife. 'I don't like the smell of death on her.'

After Louisa had had a bath and changed her dress, her father turned on her.

'Louisa, do you realise you've been stupid?'

'I haven't, Dad,' she said defiantly.

'Yes,' he nodded, 'but you won't admit it.' His anger had risen to a peak. 'For two nights I've not slept a wink because of you. I've become ill because of you.'

'Dad,' Louisa said, 'you know why Paye left here, don't you?'

'Maybe the death of his people,' Jim said. 'What has that got to do with you?'

'The soldiers went straight from here and killed his family. Do you know anything about that?'

'Nonsense. I wasn't one of the soldiers, was I? What has he told you?'

'Nothing, but I think he suspects you betrayed them. And after all the help he gave us.'

'Why?'

'I don't know.' Louisa spread out her palms. 'But he mentioned you that evening his people were killed.'

'I just told the soldiers the truth about the rice. That's all. I was just being honest.'

'Yes, but your honesty led to betrayal and tragedy,' Louisa accused her father.

'That's silly talk,' Jim shouted at her. 'And that's why you must sacrifice yourself?'

'Dad, you shouldn't have done that. After all, they were trying to help us,' Louisa said heatedly.

The quarrel between father and daughter was getting louder and louder. That was dangerous.

'That's enough, Jim, it's enough,' his wife intervened.

'Louisa must be tired and hungry.' She signalled to the other girls. They pulled Louisa to the kitchen.

Jim was still an angry man when he stormed out of the sitting room and into his bedroom. He threw himself on his bed and took an old magazine. He could not concentrate. He turned on the radio. After a long time, when his anger subsided, he fell asleep.

When he woke up three hours later, his mind was still brooding on Louisa's behaviour. There was nothing he could do about the love that had developed between his daughter and the young man, he admitted to himself. Absolutely nothing. He also realised that there was some truth in what Louisa had told him. It would be difficult to admit that, though.

◇

As soon as he got home, Paye had a bath and changed his clothes. He was back in the house he feared to live in. But there was nowhere else for him to go. If there was no safety in the church, where else could one turn?

At the church, he had heard that innocent people had been attacked and killed in embassies and hospitals. Rebels were slashing the throats of enemies and openly raping women at roadblocks. Pregnant women had been shot and their bellies ripped open. The foetuses were pulled out and tossed aside. There was a huge pile of human skeletons on Du Port road.

When Paye went to bed, he slept lightly, and woke at the slightest sound. His constant companion now was the little radio.

He was having lunch the day after his return when Louisa knocked at the door.

'Come and join me.' He spooned more rice and corned beef on to a plate.

Louisa washed her hands in the kitchen and joined him.

'Your father must be really annoyed with me,' he said as they ate. 'What did he say after I left?'

'He was mad at me, but I answered him back squarely.' She did not mention what they had actually said. 'After all, I'm back and that's the most important thing,' she added.

Paye sighed. 'The BBC announced the massacre this morning,' he said. 'Did you hear it?'

'No. If my father did, he didn't tell me.'

'Hmm,' Paye sighed again. 'We could be dead by now, you know.'

Louisa nodded. 'D'you know what my dad told me this morning? He said since I had decided to go after you without his permission, he is putting my life in my own hands.'

Paye stopped eating. 'What do you mean by that?' he asked with a puzzled face.

'That I can do what I like. He doesn't care whether I get killed or not.'

'I don't like it, Louisa,' Paye said, shaking his head. 'Does he know you're here now?'

'I told him I was coming to see you.'

'Better hurry back before he storms in here.'

'Are you giving me up too?' She sounded worried.

'No, Louisa. You know I like you very very much,

but I wouldn't like to create any problems for you at home. Your father is already angry with me.'

They had finished eating. Louisa washed the plates and left. Paye turned on the radio.

◇

It was almost dawn. Paye was already awake. In the darkness, he tossed about, his mind going over all the things that had happened in the last few days.

He was about to turn on the radio standing by his pillow when he heard a familiar but unpleasant sound. The sound of boots in the street. Were those people up to their games again? He peeped through the window and cursed silently. Soldiers combing the houses again! They were already in the compound.

Quickly he pulled on his shorts and turned the mattress upside down so no one would notice it had just been slept on. Then he slipped into the ceiling just as the front door was kicked open.

The soldiers had come again in their search for food. Holding flashlights, they called out to the occupants of the house to come out. When no one came out, they searched every room, breaking the locks on the doors. They found nothing in the kitchen except half a barrel of water and cooking pans with blackened bottoms. In the other rooms there was nothing to carry away.

'Come on, all of you, don't you see the destruction all around?' one of the soldiers said. 'This is an abandoned house. Let's go.'

The soldiers walked away, leaving behind a colleague

who had decided to use the bathroom.

'Hurry up, there's no time to waste,' one of the soldiers told the one they were leaving behind.

Lying on the beams, Paye had opened the ceiling board just a crack and was watching as they searched. It had been a very short visit this time.

Paye could still hear some noises in the house after the soldiers had gone. Someone was groaning and occasionally stamping his boots on the floor.

Paye opened the ceiling board wide, climbed on to the wardrobe and jumped softly down to the floor. Then he tiptoed to the door. There was someone in the toilet, one of the soldiers. A flashlight was showing in that room and the door had only been closed halfway.

From the way he was groaning, it was obvious that the man was unwell. He had left his gun against the wall, just outside the toilet door. Foolish, Paye told himself as he clenched his fists hard and tiptoed quietly forward.

It was an extremely long wait for Paye but, five minutes or so later, he heard a sigh of relief and a belt being buckled. He braced himself.

When the man stepped out of the toilet, his gun was not in place. But more serious than that, he did not know who booted him from behind and sent him crashing to the floor. The flashlight was sent flying to the centre of the sitting room. But it was not broken. Its light shone directly in the face of the soldier whose head had been pinned to the floor in a stranglehold.

'You killed my family, didn't you?' an icy voice said from behind the soldier's head.

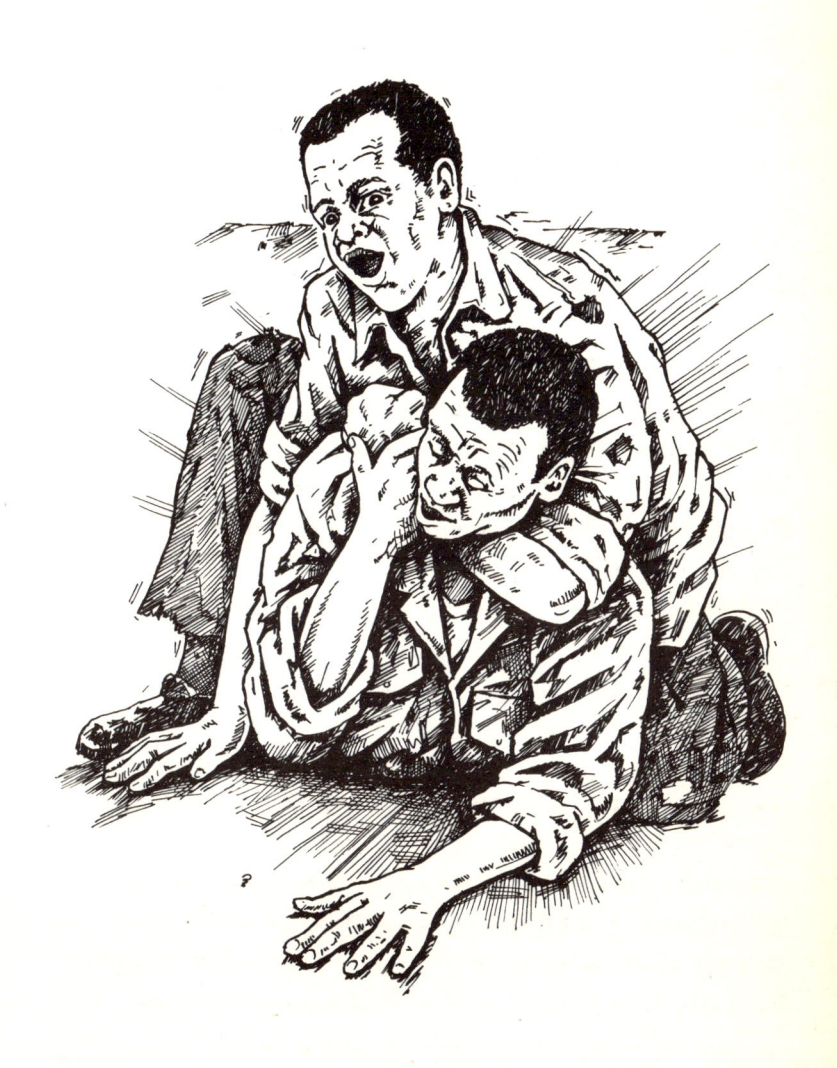

With that, Paye's anger boiled over

'I'm not one of them, please,' the soldier gasped. Beads of sweat stood on his face.

'You people gunned down my family,' the cold voice repeated.

'I don't know about that, brother.' The soldier was trying to see how he could free himself.

'What brought you here again?'

'To search for food.'

'Yes, you've come to take away innocent people's food and then kill them.'

'Brother, allow me to breathe a little,' the soldier pleaded.

'And you people massacred innocent children, old people and pregnant women at the church.'

With that, Paye's anger boiled over. Turning his face away, he jerked the neck violently sideways. He heard a crunching noise, felt the man struggle for a moment and then lie still.

Paye stood up and heaved a sigh of relief. He had got some revenge for the murder of his family.

The other soldiers in the group, eager to finish the night's operation and get back, had forgotten to look for their colleague. It was later that morning when they realised that one of their men was missing. It was too late to go back.

In the morning, there was a body lying at a street junction about a kilometre from Paye's house. It was dressed in camouflage uniform. No passer-by bothered about it or looked at it twice. There were too many corpses to bother about any particular one.

Chapter Nine

A few days later there was a welcome announcement on the BBC. The ECOMOG troops had arrived at the Monrovian port on Bushrod Island. The soldiers were pushing their way into the city. Meanwhile one of their ships was waiting to take refugees out of the country.

Paye made up his mind immediately he heard the announcement. He would get out of this wartorn country. The ECOMOG troops were coming. But that would not be a guarantee of immediate peace.

The radio had also announced that one of the three warring factions did not want ECOMOG in Liberia. They had, therefore, begun to open fire upon ECOMOG troops and were taking prisoner citizens of the ECOMOG countries. Peace was still a long way off.

That evening, Paye packed a few items of clothing into a small bag. Then he walked to Louisa's home.

Her father answered his knock at the door and only nodded in reply to his greeting.

'You want Louisa?' he asked gruffly.

'Not exactly,' Paye answered. 'I'm leaving the country tomorrow and I thought I should inform you.'

Jim had not wanted to see Paye again so soon. But the announcement of his departure came to him as a shock.

'Come in and sit down,' he invited Paye in a friendly voice. 'You mean you are going to another country?'

'Yes, sir. An ECOMOG ship at the port is ready to take people out. I'm taking advantage of it.'

'I heard the announcement. To which country are you going?'

'Any of the West African countries. The important thing is to get out of here.'

'What will happen to the house?' Jim asked.

'Well, it may be looted in my absence, but it will always be mine,' Paye answered. 'I can always come back and take possession of it.'

'And when do you intend to return?'

'I don't know, sir,' Paye shrugged. 'There's no safety anywhere, whether it's an embassy compound, a church or your own home. The country is in a mess. Since the university closed down, I don't see any future for me here. Perhaps outside, I can get my life back together again, continue my education and plan for the future.'

'Hmm,' Jim sighed, looking into the faces of his wife and daughters. 'I really was foolish not to have moved out of this city before the war got here,' he said. 'Anything can happen to us even though foreign troops are here.' He went on and on, talking more to himself than to the others.

'My greatest worry now,' he continued, 'is the cholera epidemic which has broken out. None of the hospitals or clinics is working. Thirteen people have died of the disease already. If it strikes this house, we're finished.'

Paye stood up. 'I must go now. Goodbye. I hope we can meet in better times.'

'Goodbye, young man,' Jim said, shaking hands with Paye, 'and thanks for everything.' He seemed to have softened all of a sudden towards Paye.

Everyone in the house was sad that he was leaving.

'Louisa, see him off,' Jim told his daughter.

There was no need to ask. Louisa was already standing up. She accompanied Paye out.

Back at his place, the two exchanged few words. Louisa sat sobbing for the best part of the hour that they spent together.

'Paye, you're a man now, you're bold and strong. Why do you have to leave?' she asked through her tears.

'Stop sobbing, Louisa. I have to leave. I've had too much of the war, that's all. But I'll come back and I'll write.' He kissed her on the cheek. 'If you don't see me tomorrow, it means I've gone.'

Louisa turned quickly and left the house, sobbing.

◇

By six o'clock the following morning, Paye was ready. He had eaten the rice left over from the previous day. He locked and boarded up the windows. Then he climbed into the ceiling and put the radio and other valuable items there. He took the envelope containing the money Paa had given him for safe keeping. Then he took his most prized possessions – his high school certificate and his documents from the university.

Down on the floor, he put the papers in a transparent polythene bag. He removed the trousers he was wearing and sewed the bag inside one leg. Then he put the trousers back on.

With his travelling bag hanging from his shoulder, he was securing the doors with a hammer and nails when Louisa's father walked into the compound.

'We've decided to go with you,' he told Paye. 'Once we get out of this country we will find our way to Freetown. We'll stay there and come back when things get better.'

Paye was surprised but he did not show it. 'So you're ready?' he asked.

'Almost,' Jim said, 'if you'll come and wait a while for us.'

Paye finished nailing the doors and went along with him.

By eight, Jim and his family were ready, each of them carrying a bag. They locked up the house. Then they began the long trek to the port on Bushrod Island.

Hundreds of people were also heading for the port. They all joined up to form a large crowd. There was no trouble, at least not until they got to the Johnson Street junction. The open truck screeched to a halt in front of the advancing crowds. Tied to its bumper was a human skull.

There were several men aboard. Each of them held a gun with its muzzle pointing upwards. They were wearing red headbands. Some of them had grenades hanging from their belts like decorations. They looked well fed, but there was a furtive look about them, as if they were escaping from something.

None in the crowd could tell which of the three

fighting factions these men belonged to. But once they held up their guns, everyone knew they were part of the war.

One of the men looked down at the crowd. 'Where are you going?' he shouted.

'The port!' many in the crowd shouted back.

'You mean you're leaving the country?' the man shouted again.

'Y-e-e-s!' the answer came.

'You're deserters, eh, rats leaving a sinking ship. Whose country is this?' he asked getting angry.

The crowd kept quiet. The women and children among them moved closer together for protection.

'I asked whose country this is? Go on, turn back! This is your country and you'll stay here!'

No one in the crowd moved.

The man signalled to his colleagues. The men spread out inside the open vehicle, levelled their guns and fired into the crowd.

People screamed and fell. The crowd broke up. People ran helter-skelter. Again and again the men fired at them. Then the vehicle sped off, its occupants still firing at the crowd.

Paye stepped out of the gutter and began to run. He tripped on someone and stumbled. It was Louisa's father. He had been shot in the head and blood was oozing out of his mouth. Paye kneeled by him and held him. But Jim was a dying man. As Paye held him, his body went limp. Beside him was his wife with an ugly hole in her neck. Her body lay still.

Gently, Paye lowered the dead man to the ground.

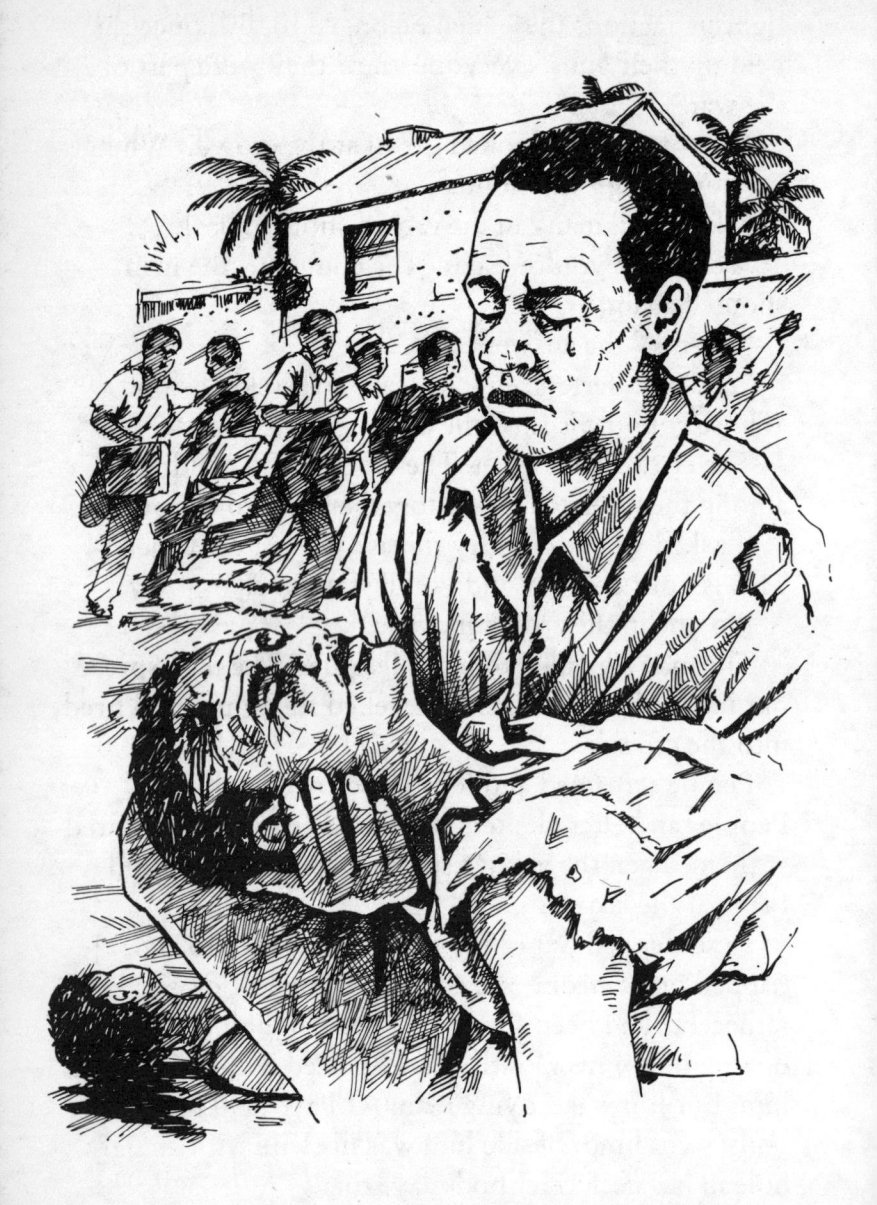

Gently, Paye lowered the dead man to the ground

Then he ran after the crowd rushing to the port. That pick-up could come back. Another could appear.

About two kilometres further on, the crowd, now considerably smaller, met the first ECOMOG soldiers. Some were on foot, others were riding in armoured personnel carriers and trucks. They were erecting roadblocks as they came along. And they were gradually pushing their way into the city.

How the crowd cheered and waved to the soldiers. Paye found himself shedding a few tears, like many in the crowd. If only they had come earlier, many thousands of lives could have been saved, Paye thought. Then it occurred to him that the pick-up must have been escaping from these advancing troops.

Now that there was some safety, the tired crowds slowed down as they approached the port.

At the port, Paye tried to search through the crowds for Louisa and her sisters. But it was no use and he soon gave up. Thousands of Liberians had come here to escape from all the horror.

The refugees began to board the ship that same afternoon. There was a scramble as they tried to get aboard the MV *Tano River*, a Ghanaian ship.

A group of young men tried to climb up the ship's anchor. They nearly succeeded. Just as they were about to reach the ship's rail, the man at the top lost his grip and came sliding down, knocking off the four people beneath him. They tumbled into the sea. All of them drowned before a boat could rescue them.

That same night, the ship set sail for Ghana. It had over six thousand refugees aboard.

Chapter Ten

Three days later, the ship arrived in Tema harbour. Its deck had been so crowded it had been impossible for Paye to go round looking for Louisa and her sisters.

The Ghana authorities had prepared a welcoming party for the refugees. A soup kitchen had been set up near the docks to give out food. An emergency medical centre treated the wounded and the sick.

A few people had died and several babies had been born during the three-day journey. As people descended from the ship, some clutching their few possessions, others with nothing, many collapsed from hunger and weakness. They were carried off to the medical centre.

It was a pathetic sight. But everybody was relieved that they had escaped from their wartorn country.

Paye, with his bag hanging from his shoulder, was standing in the food queue when he spotted Louisa in the crowds. He squeezed through the masses of people and tugged at her dress.

'Oh Paye, at last,' she said, giving a great sigh of relief and smiling happily at him. She threw her arms around him. 'I thought I'd left you in Monrovia.'

'I've been searching for you right from Bushrod Island,' he told her. He was so delighted to see her.

'Have you seen my family?' she asked him.

'No,' Paye shook his head. 'Aren't you hungry?'

'Yes, very,' she replied.

'Come on then,' he said, pulling her out of the crowds. 'Let's eat first. We'll look for them later.'

They went back to Paye's place in the queue.

After they had eaten, they got on one of the buses that had been provided. They were taken to a camp near Gomoa Budumbura, a few kilometres from Accra, along the Cape Coast road.

The camp was huge, spread out on gentle, grassy slopes. There were lots of little concrete houses as well as hundreds of tents. Paye and Louisa, being among the first to arrive, got cubicles in one of the houses.

The United Nations High Commission for Refugees, the Ghana government and several charitable organisations helped to settle the refugees. Food was distributed once a day. Everyone had enough for three meals. They were also given blankets, hurricane lamps and kerosene. There was a police post and a clinic. The only problem was that the taps did not provide water all the time, and the refugees had to go to nearby villages to get water.

Paye made the best of his cramped cubicle. It reminded him of the space behind the trapdoor in the ceiling at home. He slept for almost two days immediately after their arrival. On the third day he took a bus to Accra and changed some of Paa's money at a bank. He bought a few things for himself and Louisa.

Later that day he went with Louisa to the nearby market town of Kasoa where they bought two twenty-five-litre containers to carry and store water.

Louisa had not managed to relax since they had arrived at the camp. She searched most of the time for her family. Paye had not mentioned the scene at the Johnson Street junction to her. He felt it was too early to give her such a shock.

'Paye, I'm worried about my father and mother and my sisters,' she told him the next day when she went to his cubicle.

'Just take it easy,' he said. 'Now that we've all been registered, we'll see the camp commandant tomorrow.'

The commandant, an ex-army captain, was very sympathetic when Paye and Louisa told their story the next day.

'What's your family's last name?' he asked.

'Ackerson,' replied Louisa. 'My father is James Ackerson.'

The commandant went over the lists of names carefully, then shook his head.

'There are three Ackersons here, all men, but there's no James Ackerson among them.'

He gave her the tent numbers of the three people.

'You can ask them. Maybe they know something.'

'Thank you very much,' Louisa said.

'Check here every day. If we hear anything or if more people arrive, we'll let you know,' the commandant added.

Paye and Louisa went to talk to the three Ackersons. They knew nothing about her father.

'Where can they be?' Louisa kept asking desperately.

◇

Late that afternoon, Paye took Louisa for a walk to Budumbura village. They went to sit in the village bar.

It was a small place, and there were very few customers. Paye ordered two bottles of beer. They drank the beers quickly and Paye ordered more. He watched as Louisa drank.

'Louisa, I want you to listen to me,' he said. 'I've something to tell you.'

'Is it about my family?' she asked. 'It is. I can see it in your eyes. What's happened to them?'

'When those men in the pick-up fired into the crowds in Johnson Street, your father was right behind me. I think I heard him scream.'

'And what happened?' Louisa asked, her whole body tense.

'I think he fell.'

'Ooohhh,' Louisa wailed. 'That means he's dead.'

'I'm not sure.'

'What about m..m..my mother?' Louisa asked as she raised her tear-stained face.

'I think she fell too.'

'Oh Paye, you're not telling me everything. Please tell me what happened.'

Paye took a sip of his beer. He didn't want to hurt her, but he would have to tell her some time. He told her what he had seen at the road junction.

Tears streamed down Louisa's face. She cried so much the bar-keeper grew worried.

'What's wrong, mister?' he asked Paye.

Paye, who was in tears too, told the man the story.

'I'm sorry, my sister, I'm sorry,' he said. 'That's the bad thing about war.'

Louisa wept for a long time.

Tears streamed down Louisa's face

'Then my sisters were killed too,' she said at last.

'I honestly don't know what happened to them,' he replied. 'You remember the crowd ran in all directions. Some of them went back towards the city. Your sisters could have been among them.'

Paye took Louisa in his arms and wiped her tears.

'And you didn't tell me all this time,' she moaned.

'I ... I didn't want to hurt you,' Paye said gently. 'I was waiting for the best time to tell you.'

Louisa wept all that evening. When Paye said goodnight, he was still feeling guilty that he had told her the bad news. He was so worried that, as soon as he woke up in the morning, he went to knock at her door.

After three knocks, there was still no response. He was getting alarmed. He was thinking of breaking the door down when he heard her stirring.

'Are you all right?' he asked as she opened the door.

'Yes,' she nodded. 'Why, did you think I had committed suicide or something?'

Paye was embarrassed. 'I knew you wouldn't do that. Er, the kenkey and fried fish we had the other day, would you like some for breakfast?'

Louisa nodded.

'Well then, after you've had a bath, let's walk to the village and get some. I'll wait in my room.' He left her looking happier than she had the previous evening.

Louisa knew that she had to accept the death of her parents. As for her sisters, she could only hope they were alive.

Chapter Eleven

The poster on the camp notice board said that a large plot of land had been set aside for the refugees. Anybody who was interested could get a piece of land and cultivate it. The authorities would provide tools, seeds and fertiliser.

Paye, not used to doing nothing all day, took the opportunity immediately. He obtained a sizeable portion of land and got the necessary equipment from the commandant's office. He divided his land into six sections and used two for cabbage, two for lettuce and two for shallots.

He always left the camp very early in the morning for his garden. A nearby streamlet which emptied itself into Lake Weija provided the refugees with water for their gardens.

Louisa often came to help on the plot. She put all her energy into the gardening – forking the soil, removing dead leaves, and fetching water from the stream. Sometimes she worked harder than Paye. Paye watched her closely.

He knew that she was fighting inside, trying to forget her sorrows. They had stopped discussing their families and events back home. It did neither of them any good.

By the time they left the farm, they were often very tired. They would bathe and have their supper and then they would sit beside the Accra–Cape Coast road. They would sit for a long time, talking very little as they watched the vehicles speeding by. They would sit there until it was quite late. Outside her cubicle, Paye kissed her goodnight.

The first harvest came. It was a bumper harvest for the gardeners.

They had all worked hard. The Ministry of Agriculture vans came round to buy the farm produce. Most of the gardeners had cultivated vegetables. Paye and Louisa received over sixty thousand cedis from the sales. That evening, when he offered her half of the money, Louisa said she had earned only a third.

'Thanks, Paye. Will you take me to Accra on Saturday? I'd like to buy some clothes and visit a hairdresser.'

'You really need to see one. Your hair is getting long and bushy again,' he said. 'I'd like to get some books for myself from town.'

The very next day, they started to prepare the soil for another crop. Paye was surprised how a company secretary, used to working in a modern, air-conditioned office, could work so hard in the garden. But as he watched her from the corner of his eye, he saw something else.

He saw the curve in Louisa's body, the firm hips and the slim waist, the rounded breasts and the slim, shapely legs. The large eyes had regained their brilliance. Louisa's beauty was coming back.

Often as he watched, he would swallow and turn his eyes away before she caught him staring at her.

It was, however, not only Paye who had noticed Louisa's beauty. Many young men at the camp had noticed. Among them was Jawulu, who had decided that she deserved to have better company than that dull Paye.

Jawulu had begun to look for a way to take her from Paye. He had three friends to help him carry out his plan.

◇

On Saturday morning Paye and Louisa walked through the hustle and bustle of Accra. They went looking round the city centre with its markets and shops and offices.

Louisa had bought a skirt and a shirt while Paye had got a good pair of second-hand trousers. Then while Louisa went to get her hair styled, Paye went round the bookshops and bought three books. Louisa was waiting for him when he got back.

'That's my lady!' Paye said, giving her a kiss on the cheek. Then he caught his breath. 'You look beautiful.'

'Thank you, sir,' she said, suddenly looking shy.

'Let me get you earrings to complete your beauty.'

They went into a shop where Paye bought her a delicate pair of earrings.

'Oh thank you, Paye,' she said as she put them on.

◇

Paye had now begun to think about his university education. It was about a year since the university in Monrovia had been closed down.

'I want to begin making enquiries at the University of Ghana,' he told Louisa one evening as they sat in the shade by the main road. 'Perhaps something might come of it. If I can talk to the registrar, he can tell me.'

'Go and try,' she encouraged him. 'I'm thinking of looking for a job in Accra too. When I went to the commandant's office, I saw an advert in the papers. One of the hotels in Accra wants a secretary.'

So the following morning, they went to Accra together. They parted company at the city centre.

At the University of Ghana, Paye had to wait for half an hour before he could see the registrar.

'What can I do for you, young man?' the registrar, sitting behind a broad desk, asked.

'I'm a Liberian national, sir,' Paye began to introduce himself.

'Aha,' the registrar interrupted, guessing the purpose of the young man's visit, 'and you want admission here.'

'Yes, please.'

'A few of your people have been here to make similar enquiries,' the registrar said. 'The Ghana government, the Christian Council and the university authorities are making the necessary arrangements. So please give us some time. You were at the University of Liberia?'

'Yes, sir.'

'What where you studying?'

'Computer engineering.'

'Do you have any papers to prove it?'

Paye handed him his papers. He had his high school certificate, his university transcripts and identity card, as well as recommendations from his department.

The registrar studied them carefully.

'That's very impressive. You've done well,' he said, nodding at Paye. 'You were in the second year?'

'Yes,' Paye answered.

'Go to Room 106 and see the assistant registrar there. He'll take down your particulars. Meanwhile you should come and check every week. Something might develop in the next month.'

'Yes, sir. Thank you, sir.' Paye said.

◇

'Hello, sister,' someone called from the crowd as Louisa walked from the Black Star Hotel towards one of the bus stops in the centre of Accra.

She stopped and looked at the caller.

'Hello,' she said, not recognising the face.

'You're at the camp, aren't you?' the young man asked in a friendly manner.

'Yes, are you there too?'

He nodded. 'I came to look around town. I'm Jawulu. You're Louisa. I've seen you around the camp.'

Louisa felt relaxed now. 'I was just doing the same thing,' she told him. 'I'm on my way back to the camp now.'

'Do you mind if I join you? I was just about to catch a taxi.'

They walked along together, making conversation as they went. Jawulu got a taxi which took them to the Kaneshie market. Near the market was a huge lorry park.

'It's a really hot day, isn't it?' Jawulu said.
Louisa agreed.
'Let's go and have a soft drink or something,' he suggested.

She saw no harm in the invitation. She was feeling very hot and thirsty.

'Thanks a lot, Jawulu,' Louisa told him later as they walked into the camp. It was about four o'clock. Louisa went to change into her working gear and went straight to the garden.

Jawulu had paid the fares and bought her a soft drink and a meat pie. He had looked as if he had a lot of money to spend.

For Jawulu, the important thing was to make her acquaintance. He knew her name and room number even before the meeting in Accra. Now he had an excuse to visit her.

◇

Louisa was busy watering the plants by the time Paye arrived.

'How did it go?' she asked him.

'There's some hope,' Paye said, taking the watering can from her. He told her what had happened.

'It looks as if I might be lucky too,' Louisa told him. 'I saw the manager of the hotel straightaway. It's called the Black Star Hotel. It's very nice. He asked to see my papers and I told him I had left them all at home in Liberia in my hurry to get out.'

'What did he say?'

'Well, he gave me a practical test in typing and shorthand. He also got me to operate a fax machine and a computer.'

'How did it go?'

'Quite well. You know, I've been out of practice since the war began, but it all came back to me. He told me to check in a week's time.'

'That's terrific,' Paye said. Then he went down to the stream to fetch more water. Louisa began to fork under the cabbage plants.

Chapter Twelve

'My goodness, Jawulu, that girl is an eyeful, especially with that hairdo,' Talu said as he sat on the grass in front of the camp with his three friends.

'She's easily the most beautiful woman in the camp,' Tom agreed.

'The trouble is that she's always with that Mano guy,' Dehnla said. 'What do they call him? Paye?'

'They're either on the farm or off to the city together,' Talu said. 'And in the evenings, they sit in the shade by the road.'

'It's silly!' Tom exploded. 'What does she see in that fellow? He's no more handsome than you, Jawulu. And besides, your pockets are heavier. You'll definitely make a better partner for her.'

'What's more, she's a Krahn like us,' Talu added. 'Isn't it stupid for her to get stuck with a Mano?'

Tom nodded in agreement. 'We must find a way of splitting them up.'

Jawulu sat listening to his friends. He plucked a blade of grass and chewed on it thoughtfully. He had been a university student back home and the spoilt son of a rich businessman. His father had been taken from their home during the night by rebels and shot along with many others because the rebels suspected them of being informers.

When the ship had berthed at Bushrod Island,

Jawulu had told his sisters and brothers that they should all leave Liberia. But they had decided to stay on. Jawulu had, therefore, left them behind. He brought quite a bit of money and had quickly made friends at the camp.

He had started casting his eyes around as soon as he got settled at the camp. Louisa had a rare beauty, he had noticed. He would have moved heaven and earth to get her, and he spent many sleepless nights thinking of her.

'Jawulu, what does she do when you try to make conversation?' Tom asked, scratching his head.

'Apart from that day I met her in town, she just says a word or two, makes some excuse and goes off.'

'Does she smile?' Tom still asked.

Jawulu shook his head.

'So she doesn't encourage you in any way?'

'No.'

'Well, gentlemen, this is getting beyond a joke,' Tom went on. 'There's a saying that when persuasion fails, force is the only answer.'

'That's right,' Talu agreed.

'So it's simple. Either she leaves that Mano, or we make him leave her,' Tom said.

'Let's leave the girl alone,' Talu said. 'Let's threaten the guy. If the four of us have a little talk with him, he'll leave her in a hurry.'

The others agreed.

'So, Jawulu, take it easy,' Tom said, patting him on the shoulder. 'We'll never allow the beauty queen of the camp to fall into Mano hands. Krahns for Krahns, Manos for Manos,' he ended.

'Remember, you haven't told us what our prize for rescuing is yet,' said Dehnla, who had been quiet for some time.

'Let's go to the village bar then. We can begin today,' Jawulu suggested, feeling in his pockets.

The friends stood up, brushed the dust from their clothes and walked towards the bar.

The camp was very warm. Louisa had been sweating so much in her room that she had decided to sit outside. There were quite a few others sitting in the open enjoying the breeze.

She went over what had happened during the day. She had gone to Accra with Paye. There they had parted company, Paye going to the university while she went to find out the result of her interview. She had been lucky. As soon as she got to the Black Star Hotel, she was given a letter of appointment. She was to begin work the following week. It really was a marvellous opportunity. She felt very excited.

Paye had been asked to go for an interview the next morning. Louisa felt that the future was beginning to look a lot brighter.

Something else had happened. As Louisa was greeting the girls at the hotel reception counter on her way out, a handsome young man called to her.

'I overheard you talking to those girls,' he said, smiling in a friendly way. 'You're a Liberian, aren't you?'

'Yes, how did you know?'

'From your accent. I'm a Liberian too. I'm here on business. I'm staying in the hotel. Smart is my name. Are you staying here too?'

'No, I'm coming to work here, starting next week,' she replied.

'Doing what?' Smart's eyes had checked her fingers to see if there was a ring.

'The manager's secretary,' she replied.

Louisa studied him. He was about thirty, well-shaved, very polite and very friendly. He wore an elegant, London-cut suit. He looked like a man who liked to dress well.

'Good,' he said. 'I'm going to be here for the next week or two. Give me a ring when you begin work.'

He wrote his room number on a business card and gave it to her.

'Where are you staying at the moment?' he asked.

'At the refugee centre at Gomoa Budumbura,' she told him.

'Well,' he said, looking at his watch, 'I'm not in a hurry. I could drive you there.' He led her to a hire car in the car park.

Smart had been very friendly and very open. On the way to the camp, he had told Louisa that his young wife had died two years ago. Although he was quite well off, he was very lonely. He was looking not just for a companion but a wife.

Louisa felt some sympathy for him. She promised to get in touch with him at the hotel. She knew there was no place in her heart for him. Her love for Paye prevented that.

Louisa looked up at the sound of footsteps, the day's events forgotten when she saw Jawulu. He frightened her a little.

'Hello, Louisa, aren't you asleep yet?'

'It's too hot inside,' she said.

'It is a bit hot,' Jawulu said. 'I've just been taking a stroll,' he went on, hoping to be invited to sit down.

'Oh please, go on with your walk. Don't let me stop you.'

'Louisa, you talk as if you don't want to see me. Do you have something against me?'

'I've nothing against you. I hope we're friends.'

'We are, but I thought you would come and see me once in a while.'

'I can't. I've got a boyfriend,' Louisa said bluntly.

'Yes, I know, but that doesn't mean you can't see me occasionally,' he smiled at her.

Louisa yawned. 'I know exactly what you mean. I think you should try to find that kind of girlfriend somewhere else.'

'I don't care for anyone else. It's you I want,' he said.

'You're just being silly,' Louisa said. She yawned again and stood up. 'Goodnight.'

She went into her room and locked the door.

Jawulu walked away feeling foolish but also angry. How dare she speak to him like that.

◇

The camp had been a very peaceful place. There were Kissis, Krahns, Krus, Gios and Manos from Liberia all mixed together. They lived in perfect harmony, with none of the ethnic conflict which was raging back home.

The people understood why. They all wanted peace

and safety, so there was no point in fighting. In any case, the commandant and his men would not tolerate any troublemakers.

The first trouble took place a little way from the camp. Very few people got to know of it.

Louisa had started work. She left the camp early and came home late. Paye had gone for his interview and was waiting to hear if he could start to study at the university. While he waited he worked in the garden.

He was digging under the lettuce plants before watering them late one afternoon when four young men approached him.

'You're Paye, aren't you?' one of them asked.

Paye nodded slowly. 'Can I help you?' He knew they were from the camp.

'Yes,' Tom answered, 'we want you to stay away from that Louisa girl.'

'Why?' Paye asked calmly.

'Find out the answer yourself!' Talu shouted at him. 'Mister, if you want to go on breathing, just keep away from that girl.'

Paye stood up slowly. He took a deep breath and looked at each of the four young men, sizing them up. Louisa had told him about Jawulu, but he did not know Jawulu had three bodyguards.

'Who made you the matchmakers of the camp?' Paye asked them, getting angry now. 'Are there no other girls in the camp?'

'Just wait and see,' Dehnla said. The four men looked as if they were ready to fight. They each took a step forward.

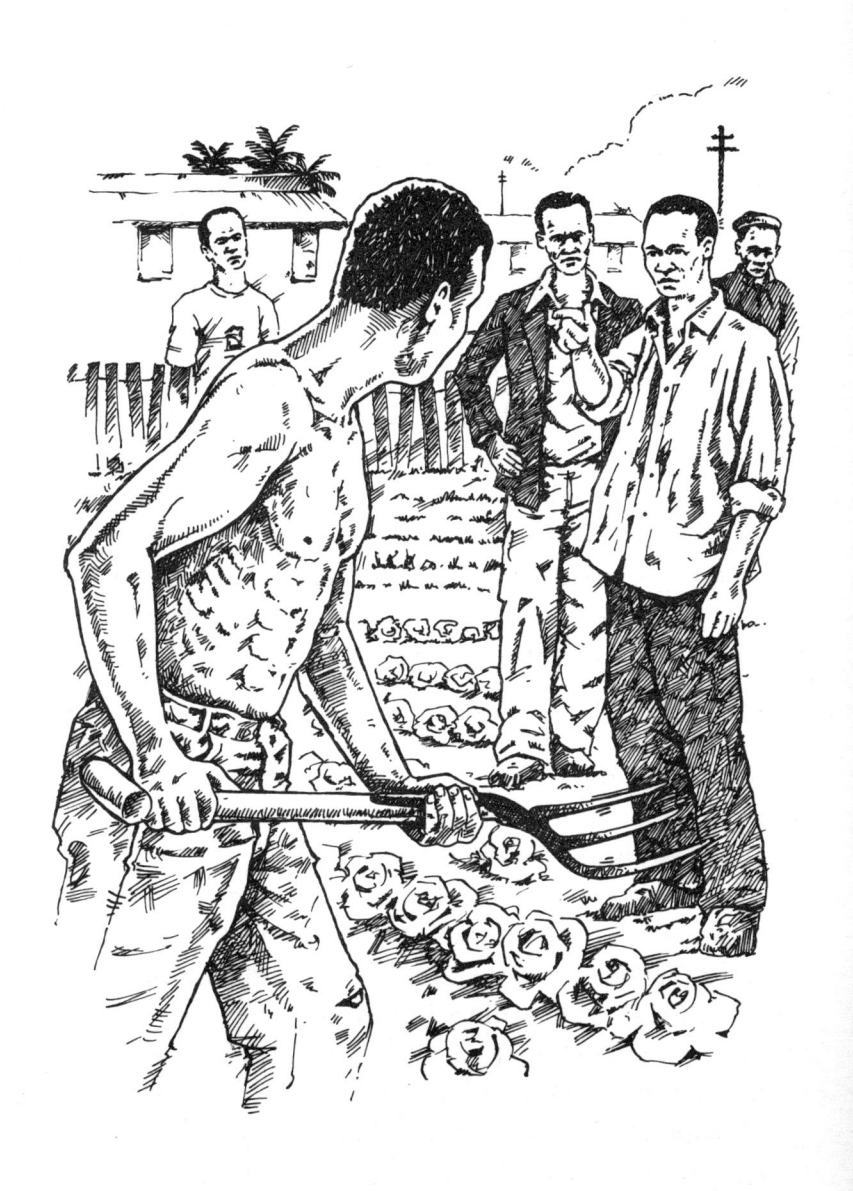

He looked at each of the four young men, sizing them up

'I'm a quiet person, but if you push me, I'll let you have it,' Paye warned them. He dropped the garden fork and tightened his fists. The sweat glistened on his bare, muscular body and there was a hard grin on his face. It was a sight Jawulu did not much like.

'Take our advice and stay away from that Krahn girl, or you'll have yourself to blame,' Tom threatened. 'Go and find a Mano girl.'

'You're a crazy bunch,' Paye said, tapping the side of his head. 'If you people are serious take another step forward. Then I'll tell you whether or not I'll stay away from Louisa.'

Jawulu stood back and urged his friends on. They did not move. Crouching low, Paye dashed forward. The three jumped quickly to one side. But Jawulu was clumsy. He tripped against one of the vegetable beds and fell heavily. Paye grabbed his shirt collar and pulled him up.

'Got you!' he snarled in Jawulu's face. 'So you want my girl, do you?'

'Have you heard me say a word since we came here?' Jawulu asked timidly.

'Look, you see this mark here?' Paye pointed to his temple. 'It's a bullet mark. I could have fought in that stupid war but I refused. And I'll have none of that nonsense here. Do you understand?'

Jawulu did not answer. It was clear that he would not fight. Paye released him.

Jawulu joined his friends and they walked away giving angry looks over their shoulders. There was a final word of warning from Tom.

'We'll get you one way or another!' he shouted. 'You won't have the girl.'

That night, as Jawulu lay on his blanket, he was still convinced that Louisa was a woman worth fighting for. The problem was he had no fighters to help him.

◇

Louisa had found it inconvenient staying so far away from the centre of Accra. She had, therefore, decided to look for an apartment at Osu near the city centre.

Paye had been admitted to second year in the University of Ghana. He was very excited. He was moving out of the camp to stay on the university campus the next day.

He had put a friend in charge of his garden. But he would come at the weekends to see how the crops were doing.

He was walking from the commandant's office when he saw Jawulu walking alone.

'Hey, Jawulu!' he called.

Jawulu began to walk faster.

'What's wrong?' Paye called in a friendly manner. 'Don't you want to be friends?'

'What is it?' Jawulu stopped.

Paye put his hand on Jawulu's shoulder.

'I didn't mean any harm the other day,' Paye apologised. 'I was just defending myself.'

Jawulu looked surprised but he still did not speak.

'Let's go over there and talk,' Paye said, pointing to a rough shed among the tents. It had open sides and had been roofed with palm fronds. A refugee family sold drinks there. Paye ordered two bottles of Coca-Cola.

'Jawulu, don't you think it was a mistake, coming to warn me like that?'

'I regret it now,' Jawulu said weakly.

'You should, because the camp has enough women for everyone. You see, whether we're the same ethnic group or not, we're all Liberians. There's no reason why we should fight. Don't you think so?'

Jawulu nodded. 'I suppose that's true.'

'If there had been this kind of understanding at home, there wouldn't have been a civil war,' Paye continued. 'Anyway, what did you do before the war?'

'Studied at the University of Liberia.'

'You mean it?'

'Sure, I was studying history and political science.'

'You see, we were students in the same place,' Paye said. 'Your three friends too?'

'No,' Jawulu said, 'I met them here.'

'Well, I was doing computer engineering. Have you made any effort to continue your education here?'

Jawulu shook his head as if he was not interested.

'You've been wasting your time,' Paye said.

'Why?'

Paye told him why. 'I'm moving to the campus tomorrow. Did you bring any papers?'

'Yes, they're in my room.'

'Good. Tomorrow we can go together. With a bit of luck you'll get in and you can start your studies again.'

They sat chatting for some time. By the time they left the shed, they had almost become friends.

Chapter Thirteen

It was late one afternoon. Paye sat at a table near the swimming pool of the Black Star Hotel. He watched as the hotel guests swam and played in the water. He had rung Louisa from the reception desk to say he was around and she had asked him to wait for her at the pool.

Knowing that he was coming to one of the best hotels in the city, he had put on his best clothes. It was just as well he did. Louisa had told him that the hotel's guests were mostly foreigners and that it was very expensive. No wonder, he thought, even the waiters were well dressed.

The hotel was a fifteen-storey building with acres of tinted glass. It looked marvellous. There were coconut palms and tropical shrubs to make the hotel into a mysterious paradise. On one side of the wide grounds, some of the guests played lawn tennis while others swam or played ball games. On the other was a casino and two magnificent restaurants.

As Paye sat watching, a waiter came up to him with a glass of beer on a tray.

'I haven't ordered anything yet,' Paye said.
'You are Paye, aren't you?' the waiter smiled.
'Yes.'
'Madam Secretary ordered it for you.'
'Fine, then put it down,' Paye said, crossing his legs and beginning to feel important.

'Madam says she'll be with you soon.'

'Thank you.' Paye pressed a fifty-cedi coin into the waiter's hand. He took the beer and began to sip it.

Fifteen minutes later, Louisa walked smartly to his table.

'Hi, Paye!' She took a seat opposite him.

'You're supposed to be working, aren't you?'

'I've just closed.'

'You look every inch a secretary now, very smart, very businesslike. This is where you belong, not the camp farm.'

'Don't tease me, Paye. Do you like this place?'

'Very much. It's splendid.'

When he finished the drink, they took a taxi to her little apartment at Osu. It was on the second floor of a block of flats. It had two rooms. She had placed a double mattress in one of the bedrooms. In the other there were four plastic chairs, a table and a small gas cooker. That was all she had.

Paye drank a glass of water at the kitchen tap and drew up a chair as she began to peel yam for their supper.

'Furnish this place a little more, and I can come and spend the weekends here,' he said.

'Sure, you can take a rest from all that studying. I'd forgotten to ask you about your studies. How are they going?'

'Not badly. But I've had to repeat the second year. The course is about the same as the one at home. But I've had to work harder. My brain seems to have gone rusty.'

'It hasn't gone rusty. Just try and work harder.'

'I will.'

'I wish you were in your final year,' Louisa said. She lit the cooker and put the slices of yam in a pan.

'Why?' Paye asked her.

'Then we wouldn't have to wait so long to marry. But there's nothing to prevent us from marrying now, is there?' she asked, looking into his eyes.

'It's too early to think of marriage, Louisa.'

'Not for a woman of my age.'

'Are you getting impatient already?'

'N-no, but you see, at twenty-four, I'm not a child any more and the earlier we marry the better. Besides, some of the men have started to worry me.'

'Please get this marriage thing out of your mind for a little while. Remember you've just started work.'

'I know,' Louisa said, 'but if I even had a ring on my finger to show them.'

'That's easy. We can buy any ring and put it on your finger for everyone to see that you're engaged.'

Louisa had been stirring the stew. She paused and looked into Paye's face.

'You want to cheapen me? You think I'm a cheap woman to wear fake rings?'

'You're getting angry over nothing. Do you want me to propose marriage to you right here and now? Is it because your boss has been making advances?'

'No, he's not that type of boss.'

'Well, I'll have to think about it,' Paye said.

That ended the talk about marriage. But as they ate, he could see that Louisa felt hurt that he would not talk marriage.

'When are you coming to visit me on campus?' he asked her.

'I'll be there on Sunday afternoon,' she answered.

After they had eaten, Paye went back to the campus, but he was a worried man.

◇

'Well, Louisa, I've told you everything about myself. It's your turn. But first, tell me whether or not there's a man in your life. I haven't seen a ring on your finger.' Smart poured some of the chilled wine into Louisa's glass and topped up his own.

'I have a boyfriend, but —' Louisa wiped her lips with a napkin.

'But what?'

'He's not interested in marriage.'

'Then forget him, he'll only waste your time,' Smart said.

It was in the evening. Smart and Louisa were eating dinner at the Black Star Hotel. Louisa wore an attractive blue skirt, a crimson blouse and a broad, black belt. Smart was wearing a sports shirt and cream-coloured trousers.

At first Louisa had only regarded Smart as a good friend. But as the days went by, she felt herself drawing closer and closer to him. Smart was handsome, polite and rich.

'You don't even need to furnish your apartment,' he said. 'It'd be a waste of money.'

'Why?' Louisa asked.

'Come and stay with me at my new place at Tesano. It's nice and comfortable. You'll love it.'

'Hmm,' Louisa sighed, feeling greatly tempted. 'That's a very different matter.'

Smart was a director of a multi-national company. He was in charge of West Africa. And she knew that he could take good care of her.

As they ate, an attractive, well-dressed woman walked in. She tapped Smart on the shoulder and pretended not to have seen Louisa.

'Excuse me a minute,' Smart said. He went out with the woman and came back a few minutes later.

'Who's that woman? She didn't even have the courtesy to greet me,' Louisa said.

'Sorry about that,' Smart apologised. 'She's the daughter of a friend. She had a message for me.'

Louisa nodded, but the woman's behaviour was not that of a friend's daughter. The meeting left a question mark on her mind.

'What's your programme for Saturday?' Smart asked her.

'I'm free,' Louisa replied. 'I'm going to visit a girlfriend at the refugee camp on Sunday,' she lied.

'That suits me fine. Join me for shopping in the morning. You can pick up a couple of dresses and a swimsuit. Then we can go for a swim in the afternoon. Is that OK with you?'

Louisa nodded. 'Yes, I'd like that.'

Smart drove her back to her flat at about eight-thirty. He kissed her lightly on the cheek and waited as she climbed up the stairs to her flat. Then he drove off.

He kissed her lightly on the cheek ...

Under one of the shade trees that surrounded the block of flats, a young man had been sitting on a cement block for so long that his buttocks ached. He saw a large car stop, saw a man kiss a woman and watched in open-mouthed amazement as Louisa went up the steps.

Paye had meant to give Louisa a little surprise. He had ended up having a shock. He walked slowly away, his mind full of unpleasant thoughts.

◇

Paye climbed wearily up the broad staircase that led to Cocoa Hall.

'Key for room AB 101, please,' he told one of the porters on duty.

'Paye, eh?' the porter asked, and without waiting for an answer, said, 'Someone was here looking for you.'

'What was their name?'

'Jawulu, also a Liberian.' The porter handed Paye a key and a note.

'Thank you,' Paye muttered, sucking air through his teeth. He did not particularly want to be reminded of Jawulu at this time. The incident at Osu had given him a big enough headache for one evening.

Paye decided not to go to his room now. The other porter was sitting on the staircase. Paye went and sat with him.

'My friend, you are usually so cheerful, but tonight you look worried. Why is that?' the porter asked him. 'Are you thinking of your people back home?'

Paye shook his head. 'It's my girlfriend. She's given me a nasty shock.'

'Is she here in Ghana?'

'Yes.'

'What did she do?' the porter, who was called Yemidi, asked.

Paye opened out his palms.

'I don't know. But I'd like to know what you'd have done if you'd been in my place.'

'What happened?'

Paye told him what he had seen.

Yemidi shook his head. 'And you stood there watching?'

'What else could I do?' Paye asked.

'Is she Liberian too?'

'Yes,' Paye said sadly. He went on to tell Yemidi the experiences he had gone through with Louisa during the war and at the refugee centre.

'You are more than husband and wife then,' Yemidi said.

'Yes,' Paye agreed. 'So you see she has betrayed me just as easily as her father betrayed my family back home.'

'Your story is very sad,' Yemidi remarked.

'D'you think it'd be worth marrying such a woman?'

'I can't tell,' Yemidi shrugged.

'And the funny thing is,' Paye went on, 'she has been going on and on about getting married.'

'When you've only just started your studies?' Yemidi asked in surprise.

'Yes.'

'You say he was driving a big hire car, eh?'
Paye nodded.
'Probably air-conditioned?'
Paye nodded again.
'Then he might be a rich fellow.'
'Of course he is,' Paye said. 'A man who drives a huge air-conditioned car must have lots and lots of money to spend.'

'You must decide what to do with her, and the sooner the better,' Yemidi advised as he stood up and dusted his trousers.

'Thank you.'

'The chief porter will be here any moment now,' Yemidi went on. 'He must not see me sitting doing nothing. But there's an old Akan proverb.'

'What does it say?' Paye asked curiously.

'That if you wait for the roasted meat to cool, it may cool in someone else's mouth.'

Both of them broke into loud laughter. Paye left feeling a little more lighthearted.

He could not read his books that night. He lay on his bed thinking of Louisa. What did Yemidi really mean? he wondered.

Chapter Fourteen

Paye was having a siesta when his neighbour knocked at his door.

'You have a call on the intercom,' the student told him.

Paye hurried to take the call. It was Yemidi the porter.

'You have a beautiful visitor here, Paye.'

'Thank you, I'll be right down.' Paye quickly rinsed his face, put on a shirt and went down to the porters' lodge. It was Louisa. She smiled at him.

'I haven't kept you waiting, have I?'

'It's all right, I've been admiring your hall,' she said.

Paye held her hand. 'Thank you, Yemidi.' He led Louisa away.

'That's a beautiful dress you have, Louisa.'

'I'm glad that you like it. I get an allowance at the hotel for clothes,' she lied. The dress was one of those that Smart had bought her the previous day.

Phe-e-e-ew! A shrill whistle rang out from a balcony. Then there was another. Soon the hall was echoing with whistles and giggles and catcalls. Students, eager for some excitement on a Sunday afternoon, rushed out to their balconies to see who was passing.

Louisa felt embarrassed. She held on tighter to Paye as they walked through the courtyard.

'What's all this for?' she asked quite innocently.

'Never mind,' he told her. 'That's how we greet female visitors, especially if they're beautiful.'

Louisa laughed lightly and immediately relaxed.

◇

'Shie! Yemidi!' the other porter exclaimed. 'What a beauty! That must be Miss Liberia.'

Yemidi smiled and nodded. 'I think she must be,' he said.

'Those eyes, that nose, those lips, the hair. And look at those hips and those legs,' the porter went on.

'Shut up!' Yemidi snapped at him. 'That's enough.'

But the other porter would not be silenced.

'Yemidi, you'd have to sell all your property to buy one kiss from this one.'

Yemidi burst into a wild laugh.

◇

'You have a nice cubicle,' Louisa said when they entered Paye's room.

She sat on the only chair in the room. Paye fetched her a glass of water.

'I hope you're working really hard at your studies,' she told him.

Paye nodded. 'I am, but I have a big burden on my shoulders, you know.'

He sat down on the small bed and faced her.

'What is it?' she asked.

'It's to do with the death of my family.'

'I lost my family too, didn't I? We must put all that behind us.'

'How can I, as a man?' Paye shrugged. 'Paa worked hard to make our family what it was. I must also work hard to continue where he left off.'

'And that's why you can't marry me now?'

'Partly, Louisa. I need to pass my exams and get a degree. Listen, I love you and I want to marry you, but at the right time. Try and understand.'

'No, I can't,' Louisa shook her head. 'People have married younger than you and before they finished their studies. You seem to be afraid of marriage.'

'Who says I'm afraid of marriage? Am I not a man?' Paye stood up and sat on the writing table. 'Let's not quarrel, Louisa. You know everybody has his own way of doing things.'

'D'you know the type of woman the Japanese describe as a Christmas cake?' she asked him, not prepared to listen to his argument.

Paye shook his head.

'It's a woman who is too old to get married, like a cake which is too stale for the market. I'm twenty-four. I can't wait until I'm twenty-six or seven when you finish your course. I want security and I want it now.'

Paye got up suddenly.

'Sorry,' he said, 'I've been a bad host. I'll get us some drinks.'

He went down to the hall shop to get drinks. As he walked back, although he hoped there would be no more talk about marriage, he felt that Louisa had not finished.

He opened a bottle for Louisa. There came another bout of giggles and catcalls from the courtyard.

'That must be another female visitor to the hall,' Paye remarked.

Louisa took a sip at her bottle and started to talk again.

'I haven't forgotten how you sacrificed for us back home. The bullet mark on your forehead is a sign of your sacrifice. I don't expect you to have enough money as a student. I'm prepared to help you with money and to bear the full cost of our marriage, I mean the rings, our clothes and whatever else there is. I've discussed it with my boss. He says the hotel will be prepared to give a full reception for twenty people at no cost to us.'

Paye scratched his head. The bait Louisa was throwing out did not attract him at all. There were too many other things.

'Tell me, Louisa, is there another man in your life?' he asked in a serious tone. 'How about the man with the big car who kissed you in front of your apartment three nights ago?'

'Who told you that?' she asked in surprise.

'Who told me? I was there. I saw everything for myself. I was sitting under one of the trees. What do you have to say?'

Louisa quickly pulled herself together.

'Yes, there is someone, but he's just a friend.'

'A friend indeed,' Paye said, nodding slowly. 'Now I'm beginning to understand you. You see, we're here all alone,' he went on, 'no parents, no relatives, nobody to control our lives. I could have taken advantage of that. You understand me?'

Louisa did not answer.

'But I didn't. Why? Because I love and respect you, Louisa.'

'Well, I'm for marriage, it's as simple as that,' she shrugged. 'If you won't marry me now, don't blame me if you hear someone else has.'

'I can see you want to leave,' Paye muttered. 'When you arrived here, I thought it was going to be a happy afternoon for us. But you only came to quarrel.'

'Paye, please see me out,' Louisa said impatiently.

He stood up abruptly. 'Let's go,' he said.

◇

'Hey, Paye!' Yemidi shouted, his hand cupped around his mouth. Paye was returning to the hall after seeing Louisa off.

'What is it, Yemidi?' he asked.

'So that's the girl you told me about.'

'Yes.'

'No wonder she rides around in air-conditioned cars. This one is fit to ride with millionaires and kings.'

'Don't talk as if she was a goddess.'

'She's certainly not a goddess,' Yemidi said, 'but you, Paye, do you have a car or motorcycle?'

'No.'

'You don't even have an ordinary bicycle. How can you hope to have such a woman?' Yemidi broke into a long fit of infectious laughter. The other porter reeled about with laughter. Paye, upset as he was, joined in.

'Come, I'll tell you,' Yemidi held Paye's hand and led him to the far end of the broad stairway.

'Paye, we're friends, aren't we?'

Paye nodded.

'Well listen then. I've been a porter in this hall for over six years. I've seen hundreds of women enter and leave this hall. I know the problems some of the most brilliant students have. Some have not survived the first year because of women.'

Paye sat silently.

'You have a big assignment ahead of you. You've told me all your people are dead. Isn't that right?'

'Yes,' Paye answered.

'That means you need a degree and you cannot afford to fail.'

Paye nodded in agreement.

'Now, there are one of two things you must do if you want peace of mind to study. Either you marry her or forget about her altogether.'

'Why do you say that?'

'You'll never have peace of mind if you keep her as a girlfriend. She's the kind of woman men will dream about and fight over. That's the advice I have for you.'

'Thanks.'

Yemidi patted Paye's shoulder and went back to his counter at the porters' lodge.

Paye slowly walked down the stairs and strolled towards the fields behind Legon Hall. A football match was in progress.

◇

That night. Louisa lay tossing and turning on her mattress for a long time. A friend she had made at the hotel had been urging her to forget Paye and marry Smart. The friend argued that with Smart she could live comfortably for the rest of her life, and that was what every woman wanted.

Louisa could not be sure if she wanted comfort without a bit of effort. If she waited for Paye, they could have quite a good life together. Besides, Paye could be relied upon in times of distress as he had demonstrated back home. Was Smart capable of doing that? she asked herself. Smart also seemed to smile too much at the ladies.

She still loved Paye, but the problem was that Paye would not commit himself to an early marriage. Well, if that's what he wants ... Louisa turned on her side and dozed off.

Chapter Fifteen

It had been an uphill struggle for Paye as he tried to forget Louisa and concentrate on his studies. Somehow he had succeeded.

The football he played in the evenings helped him to sleep better and to work on his books. As the days passed he was able to work harder and harder. Deep down inside, however, he knew something was wrong.

He had just returned from the university library and was preparing to go for supper when he had a telephone call.

'Paye here,' he said into the handset.

'Ah, it's good you're around,' Louisa said. 'It's been a long time. I wanted to find out how you were getting on.'

'Fine,' Paye said simply.

There followed a long silence.

'Are you still there, Louisa?'

'Yes, em … Paye, I'd like us to meet somewhere.'

'What for?' Paye's voice did not sound very friendly.

'Just a chat.'

'You broke off the friendship, and now you want us to meet?'

'Are we enemies already?' Louisa asked.

'No, we're not enemies,' Paye said sadly.

'Then there's nothing to stop us seeing each other. I'm going to get married and I thought we could have a farewell meeting.'

'You're going to get married?'

'Yes.'

'Then you're as good as married. Why don't you leave me alone?'

'Well, if you feel like that, there's no need for us to meet.'

'OK, where and when?' Paye asked.

Louisa told him.

'I'll be there,' Paye said.

'See you then. Cheerio.'

Paye put the receiver down and walked to the dining room. As he ate he wondered what Louisa had to tell him.

◇

Louisa was sitting alone at the table under one of the trees at the Crazy Horse when Paye arrived. It was getting dark and the lights were on. The Crazy Horse was an open-air bar near the military hospital roundabout.

'Hello,' Paye said, pulling out a chair. There was not much cheer in his voice. His hand felt cold as he took Louisa's very briefly.

'It's nice to see you, Paye. What are you drinking?'

'A beer.'

'I'll have the same.' Louisa gave the order.

Paye immediately noticed the glittering ring on her finger.

'You're already married?' he asked, his eyes still fastened on the ring.

'No, engaged.'

'So you've moved in to live with him?'

'Not yet,' Louisa answered, 'I'll do that as soon as we're married.'

'Well, you wanted a quick marriage and you've got it.'

'It's your fault, Paye. My heart was all for you. With the death of our parents, we shared a common sorrow. I've loved you for a long time now. I thought our sorrow would bring us together in marriage. We should have married to keep alive the memory of our parents. However, you saw things differently.'

'I didn't want to rush into marriage, that's all,' Paye countered.

'I can't be sure that even if I waited you would marry me.'

'Louisa, I'm afraid you found it too easy to betray me. You remember what happened back home?'

'Aah, Paye, so you still cannot forgive my father even though he's dead? You cannot forget the past?'

'Perhaps I can forgive your father, but not you.'

'Why?' Louisa asked.

'You deserted me for wealth,' he accused her bluntly.

Louisa felt a shock of guilt.

'No, it's not because of that' she said quickly, 'I needed some certainty in life and Smart offered it. It's not his wealth,' she insisted.

'Well,' Paye shrugged, 'no matter what's happened, it's too late. Let's not have another quarrel. You love the man, don't you?'

'It's too late to ask that question. But he's nice, just like you.'

'Please don't make comparisons. Please.'

'Well,' Louisa shrugged, 'anyway the wedding is two weeks from now. Will you come?'

'Me come to your wedding?' Paye thumped his chest. 'You want to mock me?'

'Why should I mock you?' Louisa said with genuine concern in her voice. 'I thought, as a friend, you should be there.'

'I can't,' Paye shook his head.

'Well, will you have another drink?' Louisa asked, beginning to feel sorry for inviting Paye.

'No, thanks,' Paye said. 'Where can you get a taxi?'

'Near the roundabout.' She paid for the drinks.

Paye walked her to a spot near the roundabout and waved down a taxi.

'Cheerio,' Louisa said as she moved off.

'Good luck,' Paye waved briefly.

The taxi moved into the roundabout and sped off towards Osu. Louisa, sitting in the back seat, turned around and looked back. Paye was still standing there, looking at the taxi.

Chapter Sixteen

It was a Friday evening early in December. A cool, moist wind had begun to blow through the trees on the university campus.

It had been an interesting day at the university. It was matriculation day, when new students were welcomed into the university.

The welcoming ceremony had taken place at the Great Hall in the afternoon. The main items had been the speeches by the Vice-Chancellor of the university and the Secretary for Higher Education. It had been well attended by students and members of the public.

For the students of Cocoa Hall, always eager for some excitement, the day offered them a good chance to have fun. Soon after the two-hour ceremony, the drums of Cocoa Hall began to sound.

Most students in the hall, whether old or new, joined in the singing, drumming and dancing. The excitement was infectious. By early evening, the fun had turned into riotous merry-making. That was when 'ponding' began. New students were grabbed and hurled into the pond in the middle of the hall.

Paye took part in the merry-making. But he did not feel the excitement as much as he had expected. He vanished into his cubicle when it got to 'ponding' time.

As he lay on his bed waiting for supper, he thought something was amiss. For some reason he could not tell, he had been thinking of Louisa since he woke up that morning. He had scribbled a note and given it to a friend who was going to central Accra. The friend said he had delivered the note at the reception counter in the Black Star Hotel.

◇

It was eight o'clock. Smart's bachelor's night party was already in full swing. Couples danced on the terrace. Others preferred to do it quietly by the swimming pool. The cook and the two houseboys were busy serving assorted foods and drinks. Near a corner of the swimming pool, a young man was cooking a pig on a barbecue.

Smart's house was situated in one of the rich areas of Tesano. The large compound had trees, flowers and garden lights. It all looked very lively and attractive.

Guests kept arriving. Many of them were business executives who had connections with the host. Smart himself wore an immaculate Nigerian flowing gown with a cap to match. He chatted with his guests and encouraged them to eat and drink and have fun.

At eight-thirty, a taxi stopped at the gate. It did not bring a guest. The lady inside it handed a note to the gateman. It was to be delivered to Mr Smart. The taxi sped off as the gateman went to deliver the note.

'A letter for you sir.' The gateman bowed.

Smart, talking to a couple by the pool, tore open the envelope. The note was a short one. But it wiped the smile instantly off his face. Next, without a word, he walked to the hi-fi equipment and turned off the music.

'Ladies and gentlemen, I'm afraid the party is over,' he announced in a disappointed tone. The guests began to look from one face to another.

◇

Supper had been long in coming, but it was worth it. It was a special meal which all the students enjoyed to celebrate the matriculation ceremony.

The singing and dancing continued at the Cocoa Hall courtyard after the meal. Paye had just stepped out of the dining room when a group of young students surrounded him.

'He thinks he's escaped! Grab him!' one of them screamed.

'Toss him in!' another yelled.

It was useless to resist. Even if Paye did get away, they would get him another day.

Six strong students lifted him off his feet and rushed him towards the pond. Back and forth they swung him, and into the pond he went.

Paye held his breath before he splashed into the water. It felt cold and slimy with all the water plants and fish. He crawled out amid loud clapping and giggles and chanting. The six students dashed off to find another victim.

◇

Yemidi was making an entry into a notebook when he saw a woman dash through the porters' lodge into Cocoa Hall.

'Who's that woman who went in without reporting here first?' the chief porter asked.

'I didn't quite see her,' Yemidi answered.

'It might be the girlfriend of that Libe—' The other porter stopped short when Yemidi signalled to him.

'We'll have to check later,' said the chief porter.

Paye had just crawled out of the pond and removed his shirt when he saw a beautifully dressed woman dashing through the students towards him. She was about to embrace him when she checked herself.

'Paye, what's happened to you?' Louisa asked, looking curiously at Paye's wet clothes.

'I was tossed into the pond, part of our hall ceremonies today. Let's go up.'

They climbed the courtyard steps holding hands. Many envious eyes followed them as they went up to his floor.

'Did you get the note this morning?' he asked her.

'Yes, I did,' she answered cheerfully.

'And you decided to come?'

'Yes, Paye, I've broken off the marriage.'

Paye paused on the staircase.

'Why, Louisa?'

'He was too smart with the ladies.'

'What do you mean?'

'There are quite a few women in his life. What ended it all was the woman who came to insult me at my apartment just over an hour ago. She threatened to disrupt the wedding.'

'So you abandoned him?' Paye asked, smiling.

'Yes, they were at the bachelor's night when I left a note at the gate.'

'What did it say?'

'That I was sorry I could not marry him and that I was going back to the man I loved.'

'Does that mean you're —?'

'All yours,' she answered. 'And now listen to the good news.'

'Yes?'

'A letter was brought to me from the camp, written by my sisters,' Louisa said happily. 'They're in Freetown right now.'

'That's fantastic!' Paye tried to hug her.

'Mmmmm,' Louisa turned up her nose, 'Paye, you smell.'

Paye laughed with joy. 'Never mind that, let's go.' He pulled her up the stairs.

He sat her in his cubicle and rushed to the bathroom. He was returning after a quick bath when the floor telephone rang. It was Yemidi.

'Kindly call Paye for me, please.'

'Paye speaking.'

'Good. Listen, Paye. You know it's past nine o'clock. All female visitors are supposed to be out of the hall now.'

'Yemidi, can't you forget you saw her, just for one night?' Paye pleaded.

'I am prepared to help, but the chief porter himself is

going from room to room. He's coming towards your block now. What are you going to do?'

'It's all right, Yemidi, thank you very much.'

Paye dashed to his room.

The chief porter was going round because he did not trust his junior porters to do a thorough job. Yemidi in particular was known to favour his friends among the students. He often allowed them to keep female visitors in their rooms overnight.

Paye's door was wide open when the chief porter pushed his head into the room. The door was tied open with a piece of string hooked to the wardrobe door.

'Good evening, young man.'

'Nice evening.' Paye raised his head from the book he was reading. 'What can I do for you, sir?'

'Just the usual check.' The chief porter looked around the room. 'Sorry to disturb you.' He left.

Paye still sat behind his desk. A few minutes later, he heard the chief porter going down the stairs. He unfastened the door from the wardrobe and shut it, turning the key in the lock. Louisa had been standing as stiff as a tailor's dummy inside the wardrobe.

'No more obstacles,' Paye said as he held Louisa by the waist. 'No Krahn matchmakers, no company executives, no chief porters.' Louisa felt warm and soft.

'That's very true,' she said, flinging her arms around his neck.

'Louisa, I think we should marry soon. I've realised it would be better for us that way,' he said, holding her close to him.

'I don't mind waiting for you to finish your course,'

Louisa had been standing as stiff as a tailor's dummy

she said. 'I think I've been foolish to rush you into marriage.'

'No, you haven't. It's only that this cruel war has disturbed our lives. You were right to say that we must look to the future, not the past.'

Paye felt Louisa's body pressing against him, the firm breasts digging into his chest. As his hands gently caressed her, their lips met in a long kiss.

Outside, the wind gathered speed. A few heavy drops of rain spattered on the tiled roofing. Soon the world was drowned in a wild tattoo of rain. It was one of the last rains before the dry harmattan weather set in.

Discussion

1 Conflict between ethnic groups has been the cause of a number of civil wars in Africa. What can be done to ensure that this does not happen in the future?

2 Do you think that the Organisation of African Unity could do more to help in times of famine, drought, civil unrest and elections, and also with economic development in countries in Africa?

The Junior African Writers Series is designed to provide interesting and varied African stories both for pleasure and for study. There are five graded levels in the series.

Level 5 is the upper level in the series. It is aimed at more mature young adults and advanced readers who are looking for material which is challenging but still controlled for language and content.

Content The stories will appeal to anyone who wants to read about problems facing young people in contemporary society in Africa. At this level the series does not hesitate to ask readers to think hard, nor, occasionally, to shock them into looking again at what is happening around them.

Language Authors are encouraged to use language more freely and more evocatively than in the other levels. The basic vocabulary is about 2250 words, but new words, essential to the development of the story or just right to a particular situation are introduced. Every attempt is made to contextualise them and they are repeated through the story. Sentence length is less controlled, but very difficult or very complex sentences are avoided.

Dictionary Difficult words which readers may not know and which are not made clear in the illustrations or context of the story should be looked up in a dictionary. This will help develop dictionary skills and will ensure the reader's full enjoyment of the story.

Discussion At this level, discussion of some of the issues examined in the story will be much more useful to the reader than comprehension questions and activities. The discussion can be carried out in the classroom or among friends.

Other JAWS titles at Level 5

The Gold Diggers, Kwasi Koranteng 0 435 89359 9
The Money Game, Barbara Kimenye 0 435 89360 2
Cry Softly, Thule Nene, Shirley Bojé 0 435 89358 0
The Ivory Poachers, Linda Pfotenhauer 0 435 89362 9